Praise for *Unruly*

"Leaders are called upon to wear many hats and must meet high standards while also innovating new pathways. *Unruly* provides a masterful guidebook to exceeding these expectations by blasting right past conventional thinking. If you are a leader in any capacity, you need this book!"

—Cristal Gary, CEO, Meridian Health Plan of Illinois,
and former Deputy Governor, Illinois

"In a world of formulaic advice and the prescribed paths to success, *Unruly* offers a necessary look into how unconventional paths are a feature, not a bug. This book isn't about breaking rules; it's about breaking new ground. Lauren masterfully outlines how understanding the true nature of rules—as starting points rather than endpoints—can transform perceived barriers and create your own success, while lifting others up along the way. Lauren's guidebook is a must-have for entrepreneurs striving for their authentic path to success."

—Mallun Yen, Founder and CEO, Operator Collective

"*Unruly* takes us on an all-access tour of our interactions with rules. It provides a smart approach to decoding, working within, stretching beyond, and ultimately writing your own rules within which you can thrive."

—Robert Grammig, Chair and Chief Executive Officer,
Holland & Knight LLP

"For anyone frustrated by the constraints of rules and policies, this book offers fresh thinking about how to get things done. I have seen, both from the inside and the outside of the Department of Defense, the need for and the impact of the Unruly path. Lauren's approach made an outsider a trusted insider while repeatedly challenging the status quo and improving outcomes in the Department of Defense without ever breaking the rules."

—Wendy R. Anderson, former deputy Chief of Staff
to the Secretary of Defense

"Dr. Wittenberg Weiner understands—from experience at the highest levels of government and as a highly successful entrepreneur—that rules are parameters. She details in this superb volume that success depends both on understanding and following the rules *and* on figuring out when and how best to stretch those rules to their limits—or when to push to change the rules. Those who have to navigate complex rules and regulations of any kind can finally learn how to decode complexities and carve out a path to unbridled success."

—Dr. Stuart Shapiro, Dean, Bloustein School of Public Policy,
Rutgers University

"The rule of law is sacrosanct in our democracy, for good reason. In this brilliant book, Wittenberg Weiner lays out her Unruly ways to make an impact—in your business, your community, and political systems—while making the most of governing rules. She'll show you how to reach your unique breakthrough point within any system or organization."

—Jocelyn Benson, Secretary of State, Michigan,
and Author, *The Purposeful Warrior*

"Lauren Wittenberg Weiner has been quietly operating in the most elite levels of our military support structures. Her Unruly approach to business, politics, and life overall is a game-changing shift to find newfound success on every level. Lauren teaches you how to take on the status quo while staying true to your highest standards, working with intelligence, persuasion, collaboration, and the greater good as your guide. *Unruly* shows you how to do good while doing well, in any realm of your life."

—Patrick Murphy, first Iraq War veteran elected to Congress and
32nd Undersecretary, US Army

"As a Navy SEAL, I know mission outcome matters most, but mission success relies on rules, standards, and morals along with adaptability and innovation. *Unruly* leverages a special operator's mindset to complete your personal missions effectively. Lauren and her team took the Special Operations community by surprise in 2018 by winning a massive award as a non-operator and a woman, but she won them over with her authentic Unruly approach and exceeded everyone's expectations."

—Vice Admiral Sean Pybus (retired), former Commander, Navy Special Warfare Command, and Deputy Commander, Special Operations Command

"Lauren Wittenberg Weiner is smart, insightful, and always on point. She understands, as I do, that when operating in a political system where the odds, numbers, and rules are stacked against you, you must find or even create new pathways to achieve your desired outcomes. With her expert guidance, Lauren offers strategies to navigate what can feel like hostile or unfriendly terrain with minimal setbacks. Her approach will show you how to be effective and collaborative, empowering you to stand your ground, claim your space, and soar to new heights."

—Fentrice Driskell, Minority Leader, Florida House of Representatives

"As an entrepreneur, a community leader, and even as a hockey mom, Lauren Wittenberg Weiner has accomplished things others thought impossible. This book is a must-read for anyone looking to leverage their hard work and unique abilities to challenge and upend the status quo."

—Steve Griggs, CEO, Vinik Sports Group and Tampa Bay Lightning (NHL)

UNRULY

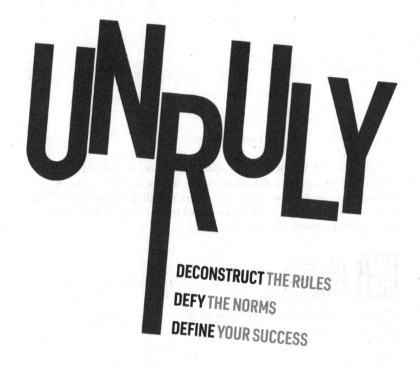

DECONSTRUCT THE RULES
DEFY THE NORMS
DEFINE YOUR SUCCESS

Lauren Wittenberg Weiner

Matt Holt Books
An Imprint of BenBella Books, Inc.
Dallas, TX

Matt Holt is an imprint of BenBella Books, Inc.
8080 N. Central Expressway
Suite 1700
Dallas, TX 75206
benbellabooks.com
Send feedback to feedback@benbellabooks.com

BenBella and *Matt Holt* are federally registered trademarks.

Printed in the United States of America
10 9 8 7 6 5 4 3 2 1

Library of Congress Control Number: 2024058125
ISBN 9781637746967 (hardcover)
ISBN 9781637746974 (electronic)

Copyediting by Scott Calamar
Proofreading by Christine Florie and Rebecca Maines
Text design and composition by Jordan Koluch
Cover design by Kathleen A. Pravlik
Printed by Lake Book Manufacturing

To Rachel and Ben . . . may you find
your own Unruly path on everything
but the rules Daddy and I set for you.

And to Jamie, my ultimate Unruly Sherpa . . .
I will continue to try to live up to your goodness
and your greatness every day. I miss you madly, J.

Contents

PART 3: CHANGE THE RULES

Foreword

I n December of 1979, as a young 1st Lieutenant, I joined the US Army's 7th Special Forces Group at Fort Bragg, North Carolina. Some years had passed since the heyday of Green Berets in Vietnam, and operations in Latin America and counterterrorism worldwide lay in the future, but "SOF," as Special Operations Forces are known, still had a distinct culture. The dedication and comradery were hugely positive, but it also had many of the more difficult aspects of most closed, elite communities. Proven competence was a prerequisite, but real effectiveness required navigating a complex web of relationships and mastering the "tribal knowledge" that governed how things got done. In uniform, excelling in SOF is demanding. As a civilian, particularly as a female small business owner, prospering in that environment is a low-probability bet wagered by the foolhardy—or those with supreme confidence in their ability to do things differently and win.

Enter Lauren Wittenberg Weiner. I had heard about this

woman who was gaining respect and getting attention for her ability to engage with intense focus while creating surprising solutions through a pragmatic yet fully fresh approach to marshaling resources. Lauren was becoming known for her ability to deliver outcomes beyond what anyone thought imaginable.

Starting any business is challenging, with the highly publicized "unicorn" billionaire experiences more entertaining than truly representative. But for a spouse living in Italy on her husband's military orders, it was even more difficult, especially when spouses can be overlooked and underestimated. Opportunities were limited, and even armed with a PhD and White House experience, Lauren had to play a new sport with unfamiliar rules, almost always competing against established firms and savvy contractors. Making a go of it demanded an unconventional, call it "unruly," approach.

My colleagues in counterterrorism operations and I found in combat that often unconventional, doctrine-defying strategy and tactics were needed to address the unique challenges of a complex fight. But I also learned that the most effective unconventional warriors begin with a deep understanding of conventional warfare. It is difficult to know when and how to color outside the lines if you don't know where the lines are or the picture being created. Lauren intuitively understood that to violate the rules, she must first master them—and she did. She also understood that simply playing the game was different than playing to win, and it is the outcome, not the activity, that measures success.

Over the years, Lauren and I have worked together transforming government bureaucracy, particularly as it relates to human capital and leadership within the government. But while naturally "unruly," Lauren sets and follows rules that establish a shared commitment across her team, and a foundation of trust with clients, customers, and partners. This seeming contradiction is anything but. It reflects her innate understanding that business and leadership aren't about operations or products, they are entirely about people. People must be developed, inspired, and led by other people who earn respect on a continuous basis. It can be unconventional, and even a bit unruly, but it's always about getting the job done that produces extraordinary outcomes, especially at times when it really counts.

Lauren has an uncanny ability to break through government gridlock. This is partly because she is smart, but also because she can see the whole battlefield and plot multiple paths to complete the mission. She does the same in the nonprofit world and in her own personal life. In this book, she presents a vision of new pathways, adaptable skills, and forward thinking that meets resistance with formidable resolve.

General Stanley McChrystal, US Army, Retired
CEO and Chairman, McChrystal Group

DOOR KICKERS, SNAKE EATERS, AND MILITARY SPOUSES, OH MY!

It is easy to be captivated by the big, swashbuckling personalities who flout the rules with impunity and find outsized success. These big personalities dominate our news feeds, our imaginations, and our modern folklore. But most everyone else colors perfectly within the lines, plods through the path laid out for them, and lives their lives without ever upending the status quo.

What if there were a third way, a hybrid solution, that allowed us to truly find our own breakout success while consistently doing the right thing?

Let's get Unruly.

Getting Unruly first and foremost means following the rules—the letter and spirit of the law, the moral path, the "do unto others" way—and then finding the space *within* those rules to distinguish yourself from the pack. The Unruly way doesn't skirt the rules, but it *will* use the flexibility within the rules to your advantage. It taps into your inner two-year-old self and asks why you have to do things certain ways, and why we can't do things differently. In doing the work to answer those questions effectively, we can plot our *own* course to our *own* version of breakout success.

GOOD GIRLS PLAY BY THE RULES?

As a kid, I was always a rule follower. I got good grades, rarely disobeyed my parents, never snuck out of the house, and diligently followed the path others set in front of me. And, truth be told, I was probably a bit insufferable to be around with my goody-two-shoes ways. All the way from preschool to college, I colored entirely within the lines, met all the marks, and succeeded by playing every game exactly as whatever powers that be set as the parameters—whether it was my parents, my teachers, or the books that I read voraciously. I believed in the rules. I was taught that they took you where you want to go and that they were made to help you become the best person possible. The rules gave me comfort, and structure, and a promise that if I did everything right, I'd make it. Wherever "it" was, I wanted to get there.

But during graduate school, I began to see a ceiling in what I could accomplish when operating within the rules laid out for me. My graduate school years were filled with powerful professors, including my own advisor who controlled nearly every aspect of my life (as PhD advisors did, by design), and some of those professors abused their power in pretty egregious ways that I'll talk about later in the book. So, by necessity, because success was for the first time no longer guaranteed by simply following the rules, I became focused on which rules were truly critical and which weren't really "rules" at all.

I didn't realize it then, but this was my first taste of getting Unruly. And as hard as it was for my good-girl self, I got a thrill out of bucking the expectations that everybody seemed to have of what I "should" do. I didn't break any actual rules—and I still don't—but I certainly broke with the "shoulds" and "oughts" and "musts" of others' expectations of me, and I found some new paths that were still moral, legal, and ethical yet turned standard convention on its head.

Look, we absolutely need rules in a civilized society. Rules can save lives—just consider our safety standards for automobiles and food and medicine, to name just a few—and they can create structure and hierarchy that allow for predictable business transactions and navigation through the world overall. Even non-rules—guidelines and norms and policies and best practices—can impose effective boundaries based on social expectations and interpersonal consequences that guide us in our lives. But overly burdensome rule structures and policies and expectations can limit our world in ways that are unnecessary and unproductive. Finding the path that allows us to stay well within the bounds of compliance and ethics but allows us to find or create our own path is the core of the Unruly journey that I'll guide you through in this book.

My experience in graduate school led me to recognize that some rules weren't black-and-white, even in commonly accepted situations. I came to understand that playing by the rules would only get me so far. My life during the rule-following days was a two-dimensional game of checkers, where I could only move in very predictable patterns, and generally only forward and backward. My real success came from understanding how to navigate with more nuance as on a multidimensional chessboard that more closely represents any "real" game that is being played, with lots of possible moves across time and space. Suddenly, I was breaking free of the constraints that had held me in lockstep with all the other high-achieving rule followers, and with each Unruly action, I was creating even more extraordinary success.

After graduate school, as I was called on to master ever-more complex rules for more complex roles, things continued to get even less clear-cut. The rules weren't always obvious. Ironically, as an avowed former rule follower, I found my first "real" job after graduate school in the White House's rulemaking office, the Office of Information and Regulatory Affairs (OIRA). We reviewed—and often rewrote—most of the rules across the federal government. Nuance became critical, and working within gray areas became the most viable, and often the only, option to achieve the goals laid out before me. Once I was able to learn to find a different path than the other rule followers around me, I found myself exceeding expectations, particularly my own.

I learned the nuances of the Administrative Procedure Act

(which is as exciting as the name makes it sound), but more importantly I learned how government rules really worked and didn't work. I learned how much gray there was in the laws passed by Congress, the follow-on rules set forth by the executive branch, and the sub-regulatory policies and guidelines that drove the business of government. As importantly, I learned where to find the source documents that drove all this regulatory mumbo jumbo as I grappled with why things had to be a certain way, especially when they seemed nonsensical. Being part of the rulemaking process freed me up to see how much gray there really was in all rules. I increasingly began to see the openings that could be utilized within the rules, and I became skilled at how to make viable and repeatable passageways through them.

In other words, I got Unruly.

THE ACCIDENTAL ENTREPRENEUR

I call myself an accidental entrepreneur. I never planned to start a company, and even twenty years in, I think of myself as more of a business or community leader rather than as an entrepreneur. The more traditional entrepreneurs I know set out specifically to start a company, regardless of the type of company it would be. They started, and sold, multiple companies, and they continued to constantly think about their next venture and how to enter a new market, scale their ideas, and exit successfully. It almost doesn't matter what their idea is; they thrive on the challenge of commercializing what they imagine.

But my path was different. As I neared the end of my PhD program, everyone assumed that I would accept a postdoctoral fellowship or seek out a tenure-track position in academia. But, in a major epiphany thanks to a wonderful mentor that I'll talk more about in part 3 of this book, I realized that I didn't want to take an academic path. A good friend was working at the White House. In conversation, I shared with him why I was not excited about academia, and he told me that I might prefer working in public policy. I had absolutely no idea what "public policy" was, but his description made it sound pretty cool—and after a brief stop at a policy research firm, I ended up working with him at the Office of Management and Budget (OMB) in the White House during the Clinton administration (and later, the Bush administration).

I was not the traditional hire at OMB, to say the least, and I had a huge case of imposter syndrome when I first got there. My job oversaw policy at half a dozen agencies at any given time—from Labor to Education to Housing and Urban Development to Health and Human Services—and at times it was part of my job to tell senior political appointees, up to and including cabinet secretaries, that they couldn't do what they were determined to do. Pretty heady stuff for a twenty-six-year-old.

My job was reviewing and rewriting the rules that came out of the laws passed by Congress. That job gave me the ability to fully understand the baseline of any rules—and further set me on the path to being able to leverage the gray areas in the rules to distinguish myself and my firm while still remaining entirely compliant with all of the legal demands and constraints.

In every interaction during my White House days, there were people in the room who had been in the government for decades, and who were often the expert on one specific policy area. I couldn't possibly rise to meet their specific expertise, but I was there to speak for and represent the policy arm of the White House. I quickly learned to leverage their expertise, without letting them drive the agenda. I was the expert in the White House processes, and I had the backing of my senior leadership, but I had to rely on the expertise of agency staff to quickly get me smart enough to make decisions on the specific policy issues they were pushing. I needed them to see me as an equal so they didn't steamroll right over me.

I realized that my lack of knowledge of certain things wasn't a problem *if* I admitted where I was lacking and sought out credible people to guide me, or otherwise found the information I needed. As I began to connect dots, I was shocked to discover that often the most confident people in those meetings were frequently the least correct. That was unexpected, coming from my rule-following, good-girl days. I quickly figured out that I needed to do the best I could with the knowledge I had—always knowing that it was likely imperfect—while steadily leveling up by expanding my capacity, enabling me to improve on prior decisions as I gained more information. I often felt like I was building the plane while it was flying (and parts were falling off in midair), and I was the one who had to keep it in the air no matter what.

I was also single when I got to DC and honestly found the dating scene to be overwhelmingly painful. Most of the men in DC were very accomplished but cocky and condescending. I went on a few dates with one guy, an aspiring politician, who told me—on our last date, to be clear—that I would make a really good politician's wife. How about I'd make a really good politician, thank you very much? I went on dates with lawyers, doctors, and Hill staffers. I even had someone try to set me up with a now-notorious politician, which I smartly turned down.

I was ready to give up on dating when I met Chuck. He was certainly accomplished, with a master's degree and a good job with the Navy, but he was decidedly different from the other guys I'd met in DC. He was genuinely impressed, but entirely unintimidated, by my accomplishments. When I handed him my slightly ostentatious, gold-foil-embossed White House business card, he told me without any reservation that he found me fascinating and wanted to take me out for dinner the next night. He still carries that card, now very tattered, almost twenty-five years later in his wallet.

The morning after our first date, I called my mom, a ritual for us after each new first date. She started the conversation with "Well, what was wrong with this one?" and, much to my surprise, I answered "Nothing." Chuck was, and still is, my biggest cheerleader. Having him always excited and supportive freed up so much of my energy, allowing me to focus on a higher purpose. As Sheryl Sandberg notes in *Lean In*, my most important career decision was in choosing who to marry, and I chose well.

But I'm getting ahead of myself. Chuck wasn't yet my husband when he got a too-good-to-refuse offer to go to Naples, Italy, with the Navy. We were just about to embark on a cruise where, as he still jokes, he was either going to propose or I was going to push him off the ship. The day before the cruise was set to leave, his former boss called to tell him about the job, and Chuck spent the entire cruise navigating the application process and negotiating the offer. And he did propose, although he forgot the ring and had to improvise with an overpriced necklace that he bought in the ship's jewelry store. Once back on dry land, we were told that we had four days to get married so that I could be included on his military orders, so off to the justice of the peace we went with our parents and a few friends, and just a few days after my thirtieth birthday, we were on our way to Italy to start our married life.

THIS ISN'T TUSCANY!

Like a good type A achiever, I did my research and found that there were two headquarter commands moving from London to Naples, with multiple high-level professional jobs open at the time, many of which I was clearly qualified to fill. I also watched *Under the Tuscan Sun* and was excited about our move to the bucolic rolling hills of Italy. But once we got to Naples, one of my husband's colleagues picked us up at the airport and immediately took us the back way (through an alley) to the new office, and I realized Naples was decidedly not Tuscany. As was common, there was a trash strike in Naples, so the dumpster at the entrance to the alley was overflowing—for three full blocks—and the garbage was on fire. It was a literal dumpster fire. Amazingly, it just got worse from there.

I was told that there was a policy on base that did not allow spouses to apply for any jobs above entry level. I was also told that I could be a secretary "until I got pregnant." Meanwhile, given my PhD, I could be an adjunct professor for one of the universities on base, but the pay averaged out to less than minimum wage when even minimal prep time was factored in; for the actual class-time hours, it was barely half as much as I had made ten years earlier as a teacher for SAT and GRE prep courses as a sophomore in college. And I might or might not be able to pick up one or more classes each semester, so it certainly wasn't enough to keep me busy and engaged, regardless.

I quickly networked my way into a contracting job, which was supposed to be working on information technology policy but turned out to be installing computers as the command moved from London into the new spaces in Italy. Anyone who knows me knows I shouldn't be doing anything to computers beyond turning them on and off, and sometimes even that is too difficult for me. Thankfully, I became close friends with one of the other contractors on base, and he saved my behind more times than I can count those first six months. I had already learned while working at OMB that support is critical, and the power of my village saved me repeatedly in that job, when by any measure I should have failed miserably.

One thing I did do, through that first six-month contract, was to meet everyone and simply solve problems for them. I figured out all the players around the base—from the facilities folks to the bill payers to the military people who made the ID cards and everyone in between. It became clear very quickly that nobody was project managing the entire move, and everyone was showing up with no coordination whatsoever, so I decided to just jump in and manage it myself. I also made it my business to know the best real estate agent who could make things happen around Naples, which was the real secret to navigating life in Italy. As people showed up, I guided them through the process and tried to make it as seamless as possible. I became the person everyone came to when they needed to get something done, and I amassed an array of the right people who were happy to help me get stuff done. It was my first lesson that the "power of yes" was critical, and it certainly confirmed that nontransactional relationships were the key to everything.

Meanwhile, at the suggestion (and with the assistance) of another military spouse on base who was a lawyer, I incorporated a company just so I could do some basic consulting work for my old agencies back in DC. She came up with the name—Wittenberg Weiner Consulting—because everyone in DC knew me by my maiden name (Wittenberg), and everyone in Naples knew me by my married name (Weiner), and it sounded bigger than just one person. Brilliant! The tagline for the company came more naturally: Putting Good Government into Practice. It perfectly communicated a continuation of the work I had been doing in the White House. I even had another friend draw up a logo featuring a stylized rendering of the White House.

Months after my job installing computers ended, I got a call from one of the first people I met on base, who we still refer to as "Saint Tony" in the firm today. He was, at the time, the head of Anti-Terrorism/Force Protection (AT/FP) for the

European region, and he asked if he could get me on contract through my company. I had no idea what AT/FP was, nor what he needed, nor how to negotiate a government contract, but if it got me into a professional role, I'd figure it out. I said "yes" first and figured out the details later—although it was critical to figure out those details and prove that my "yes" was valid. Suddenly, I was officially an entrepreneur, and Wittenberg Weiner Consulting (or WWC, as we quickly became known) was an actual no-kidding company. In short order, WWC had half a dozen military spouses stationed overseas on staff, supporting our government customers.

Eventually, over the course of almost twenty years, WWC won the largest award ever to a woman-owned business in Special Operations Command headquarters history and became one of the largest and most successful woman-owned businesses in the industry. We had $100 million in annual revenue and over 350 employees in 2022. There we were, a firm started by and with a bunch of military spouses, working directly with the elite special operators that are colloquially known as door kickers and snake eaters. Special Operations has been mostly closed to women in anything but support roles until recently (with the notable exception of Air Force Special Operations), so a woman-owned business succeeding in the space was an anomaly, to say the least.

Government contracting (which I'll call "GovCon" throughout the book) is a rule-heavy industry, with thousands of pages of rules around how the government buys from private industry, and even more unwritten rules about how to actually win that work and perform it successfully and compliantly.

Over the years, I have had the privilege to work with top performers in some of the most critical areas of government and business, from cabinet secretaries to admirals and generals to corporate CEOs and hugely successful entrepreneurs, and I realized that pretty much everything in life can be viewed as a type of game, with its own specific (and often unwritten) rules and expectations. While the written rules can be obvious (although not always), it is the unwritten rules that give us insight into how the game is truly played. But it is understanding the space within those written and unwritten rules that separates the abundant smart employees and the superstar change makers. It is in figuring out how to push on those rules through effective interpretation, and working the nuances, that reveals how to find your best path to success, how to differentiate yourself from everyone else, and how to break free of limiting conventions. And, once you've made it, it allows you to change the game for those coming up in the ranks after you so that it is fairer for all. That level of gamesmanship—the Unruly way—is what I am going to teach you in this book and what will allow you to break out to extraordinary success.

This book is structured in three parts:

1. *Learn the rules:* Before we can find the space within the rules, we have to fully understand those rules, both the written and unwritten ones. Part 1 will encourage and guide you to think about rules in a new way.
2. *Challenge the rules*: Once we understand the rules, we can really find the space within the rules to distinguish ourselves. Part 2 will show you how to push within

those rules to create your authentic path to breakout success.

3. *Change the rules*: Sometimes, the rules stop work-ing—for us or for the broader society. Rather than simply breaking the rules when they no longer work, part 3 will introduce you to the ways you can upend the rules and entirely change the game.

There are some examples of others who took the Unruly path, even if they didn't call it that, that I'll use throughout the book. These folks, most of whom I'm lucky to know and call colleagues, mentors, or friends, come from various industries—business, law, politics, the military—but all have in common a strong desire to serve something beyond themselves, a natural curiosity about the way the world works, a tireless drive to suc-ceed, and an unwavering moral compass that centers them in their approach to life.

One of my absolute favorite Unruly role models is a mil-itary spouse named Jocelyn Benson. At thirty-five, she be-came the youngest-ever female dean of a top US law school, and she quite literally wrote the book on being a secretary of state. She also ran the Boston Marathon while more than eight months pregnant, raising her to legendary sta-tus. In 2012, her husband Ryan tried to vote absentee while deployed with the Army to Afghanistan but couldn't get through administrative barriers in his home state of Michi-gan. Even Jocelyn's expertise and procedural guidance didn't ensure that Ryan could successfully vote while serving our country in a war zone.

She became the secretary of state in Michigan in 2018

and was determined to make sure that any state resident could have their vote counted while deployed in military service. She knew the voting rules better than anyone; nobody could effectively make a claim about anything voting related that wasn't borne out by facts or law without a clear, compelling, and unemotional retort from Secretary Benson, although many kept trying. She exemplified the Unruly approach you're going to learn. Among other changes aimed at safely and legally ensuring voting rights for eligible voters, she spearheaded a change in law to allow for more effective overseas voting for military members and their families, so that nobody from Michigan serving our country could be disenfranchised from their most basic rights.

START YOUR UNRULY JOURNEY

Plans are great. They help us organize and identify what needs to be done, and they give us a path to follow and the means to create a way that leads to something we want. But I have to tell you, so much more success comes from putting one foot in front of the other and banking success through one introduction, one chance meeting, one "yes," one decision at a time, with a whole lot of hard work in between. Figuring out how to capitalize on the luck you're presented—when most people don't even recognize it as an opportunity—is often more important than the best-laid plans. At any point in my professional journey, if you had asked me where I would be in five years, I would have gotten it wrong by an order of magnitude, by always underestimating where

I was going. Keeping optionality rather than rigidly following a strategic plan has always gotten me further than I could have ever dreamed.

Throughout the book, I'll distinguish between what I call "baseline success" and "breakout success." There are plenty of people who attain a modicum of success by playing entirely within the rules and never pushing boundaries. There is nothing wrong with this baseline success, if that's what you want. It affords some significant perks, honestly— less success, to be sure, but also less stress and a far better balance of other aspects in your life. Breakout success, on the other hand, leads you away from the pack to a different level of success. You can define breakout success for yourself—and your idea may look very different than mine—but it is a distinctly different level of success than you'd find by just diligently following the rules.

It takes knowing how to capitalize on the right opportunities in ways that others can't or won't to find that breakout success. At its core, the Unruly way helps you navigate this path and find those opportunities to break away from the pack. And while most of this book focuses on an Unruly professional journey, the rules can and should be applied to other aspects of your life—your role as a parent, as a caregiver, as a spouse, as a friend, as a volunteer. My Unruly professional path has taken me from psychology to policy to business and to the military space. My Unruly personal path has had me navigating aging parents and children, along with my own personal needs, and trying to sustain an enduring marriage and give back to my community in meaningful ways. This book shares what I've learned about maximizing the gifts in the gray areas of the rules and guidelines that I've collected from all those disciplines. In following the Unruly path, you can connect your own dots and put your authentic greatness to work.

Part 1

LEARN THE RULES

It's not wise to violate rules until you know how to
observe them.

—T. S. Eliot

I'M JUST A BILL

et's get Unruly!

Not so fast. I know you want to push the boundaries of the rules right away, but being Unruly starts with truly and fully understanding the rules, what they mean, and the actual constraints those rules place upon you. You cannot safely push on the rules until you fully know them. Following the rules *does* matter, and not just because of the legal and other consequences that can come from breaking the rules. The rules are part of the social contract that we all enter into as part of society, and only when the vast majority of us buy into and follow those basic rules do we have a functioning society.

The rules draw a box around the moral, legal, and ethical actions we can take as we navigate our way in the world. But that box may be a bit more like an M. C. Escher work than a four-sided right-angled shape; the lines may be wavy, and the box may be multidimensional rather than just a standard cube. And successfully navigating your way through the rules can be disorienting. The rules can be actual governmental laws or regulations, but they can also be rules from your employer or your kids' school. They can be written or unwritten, and they can have very different consequences for violations.

When you approach rules as a starting point—necessary but not sufficient for defining your path forward—you are setting the groundwork for being Unruly. Grasping what the rules are, and what they really say, lets you know where the constraints are and aren't. When you learn how to ask the right questions to understand the interpretation of those constraints and what the ground truth of the no-kidding rules are and aren't, that's when you can truly get Unruly without undue risk.

Amy is a great example of someone who took this deep dive into the rules and came out with outsize success. Amy was a lawyer with one of the big corporate law firms straight out of law school. She realized very early in her career that law wasn't for her and pivoted to pharmaceutical sales instead. She did that for more than a decade before making another huge pivot—this time to owning a laundry company.

I started hearing about this woman who came out of nowhere and landed the big laundry contract on the base in Tampa with absolutely no background in government and no preexisting relationships. Let me be clear—NOBODY comes into government contracting with absolutely no background or relationships, puts in a blind proposal, and wins a big contract. Nobody. Except Amy. Armed with a law degree and more positive energy than anyone I know, she dug into the rules and figured it out. She devoured all the regulatory language and policies around how contracts are awarded and pored through every word of the request for proposal (RFP). And she got the contract, and another one after that. This woman is the epitome of the Unruly mindset, but with a whole lot more positivity and grace than I've ever been able to muster. She figured out the rules better than anyone else, but she also makes everyone want her to succeed because she is just so easy to root for.

In this first chapter, we are going to focus on the actual legal or policy constraints that overlay whatever you're trying to do. In some industries, these are copious and complex; in my industry of GovCon, the basic set of regulations runs to tens of thousands of pages. But even in those industries with fewer regulatory constraints, a basic understanding of how the laws work and what laws apply to you will be critical if you want to push on those boundaries. And while laws are enforced at the government level, the impacts of those laws will filter down to all other aspects. Think of an employee handbook. A substantial driver of the rules in any corporate handbook are the compliance requirements and best practices from government laws. All of those rules—from the actual laws passed by Congress to the handbook for an individual company and everything else that is formal or written—are the subject of this first chapter about the written rules. So, while the unwritten rules are probably more critical than the written rules in some industries, an understanding of both is always essential for true breakout success.

As we approach these written rules, we have a layered list of questions to answer before we can use the rules to our Unruly advantage. So first and foremost, we need to ask and learn:

1. Where can we find *all* the laws, regulations, and policies that apply to a particular situation, and are there any other documents that inform these rules (guidance, best practices, etc.)?
2. What is the standard way that laws, regulations, and policies are generally interpreted and implemented?
3. Do the laws, regulations, and policies allow for any other interpretations?
4. Is there a way to take an alternate approach?
5. If the laws, regulations, and policies do not allow for our chosen path, are there changes that can reasonably and effectively be made that are cost- and resource-effective, or should we look to pursue a different path entirely?

I tend to look at everything through a "play the game" lens; even in high-stakes, deadly serious situations, such as war, there are clear "moves" we make that provoke countermoves and reactions. I've found it helpful to use this game analogy when thinking through rule-based situations to expand optionality and to challenge the status quo or accepted route, and I will use the analogy throughout the book. The rules set up the parameters of the game—whatever that particular game is. Some of the situations we find ourselves in are certainly consequential, but there is still value in seeing through a game lens. In this, the rules, both the written and unwritten ones, set forth the playing field and the basic moves you may be able to take to uncover areas of opportunity.

This book provides some lessons and a general framework for how to succeed while staying within the constraints of the rules. If you're looking for the book to show you how to cheat and avoid accountability, how to dominate your industry without regard to others, or how to get away with (literal or figurative) murder, there are all sorts of books out there for you, starting with the king of them all, Machiavelli. *This book is anti-Machiavellian.*

This book can't, and won't, teach you morality. I can't define morality for you or guide you as to what is okay or not okay in any given situation, or even overall. This book assumes you've got a desire to stay solidly within the overall laws and norms of society and are just looking to find your own authentic place within that space. It assumes that you're not comfortable screwing people over to get ahead or blatantly violating the law. If you don't already have a strong moral compass, this book will be a whole lot less effective for you. The Unruly approach assumes that you've got that strong foundation and desire to do the right thing and are looking for the tools *to be morally upright and still succeed.* This book *can* teach you how to be comfortable and maybe feel like less of a sucker for doing what is right, by following your moral compass when so many around you seem to break the rules with impunity. One of the keys to being Unruly is learning how to interpret and listen to the twinge in your gut when you may be crossing lines, and to distinguish that from the twinge you get when you're just pushing out of your comfort zone.

Look, I'm not naïve. I know there are plenty of people who blatantly break the rules. And plenty of those folks do very well in life and rarely face consequences for their actions—at least not consequences that are harsh enough to disincentivize the bad behavior. Most of the bad behavior is never discovered, and it's rarely punished effectively even when it is. So, there are people who can make the very logical choice to actively break rules, factoring in the risk and reward and recognizing that they'll likely get more than they pay out in most cases.

Regardless of the ability to get away with bad behavior, I am a strong believer that you can do the right thing and still succeed. I'm living proof of it, in fact. I have met plenty of people who succeeded—at least from a financial perspective—by breaking the rules, but I did see it often come back to bite them in the long run, even if not with legal consequences. People didn't trust them and didn't want to do business with them. They ended up with fractured personal relationships. They were always striving for more, more, more . . . and never seemed satisfied with what they'd accomplished. I'm not sure they were miserable—particularly the ones that valued money over the other things that make life even richer—but it wasn't a balance that made sense to me.

Learning how your gut can guide you in making the most of the nuances of the rules can get you to the moral, ethical, legal, *and successful* outcomes that matter most to you. But if you don't have that solid underpinning, if you're not looking to blaze the legal and ethical and moral path, there are plenty of other books that will show you how to leverage power over people, how to find the ways to break the rules, how to conquer the world by any means necessary. That's not being Unruly; that's being a rule breaker. Also a jerk. The last thing the world needs is more jerks.

NAVIGATE YOUR OCEAN

I came up through military contracting during the early days of the global war on terror, when the range of opportunities made it feel like the new Wild West. Money was free flowing, and rules were jokingly referred to as "suggestions." The movie *War Dogs* wasn't far off in capturing what many firms did in those days. Blackwater was the most notorious, and years later, I remember reading Erik Prince's memoir, *Civilian Warriors*, in horror at the way he spoke about breaking all the rules and norms as if it were no big deal. Reading his book, once I had been working within the industry for some time and had my feet solidly underneath me, I was reminded of the blue ocean/ red ocean strategic framework described by W. Chan Kim and Renée Mauborgne in their book *Blue Ocean Strategy*, where the red ocean is the crowded place in each industry where all the firms are competing, and the water is bloody red from the battles they're fighting just to stay afloat; and blue ocean is the open water, where nobody else is competing.

But what struck me about the blue ocean concept was that sometimes firms that didn't have a grasp on the rules—or a strong moral compass—got themselves into a wide-open space that wasn't legal or ethical. This was what Prince did in building Blackwater. To me, that's not blue water. While thinking about his revelations from his time with Blackwater, I realized that there was a third type of water that was even more critical to steer away from than the red water—and that was black water, where rules and ethics were flouted with impunity. Those in black water may succeed, at least financially, but success can come without navigating into black water. Understanding the rules—and the boundaries that those rules do and don't impose—is the key to sailing through blue water rather than into red or black water.

I will make the distinction throughout the book between red water, blue water, and black water. We want to stay out of the crowded and bloody red water where everyone is competing, and where everyone plays by the same standard playbook. Unruly ways can move us into happily navigating into blue water—still perfectly legal and ethical waters, but with much more room to maneuver without a crowded competition field. And this book is also written to help keep you out of the black water: the boundary crossing, the illegal acts, the unethical plays. Learning how to truly understand the rules and how they work leaves room to play in the gray areas without crossing into the black ones, so that you can stay on the right side of the rules.

The Unruly path pushes boundaries and figures out where there are opportunities in the open spaces within the rules, and the fun part of our Unruly path comes once we can start playing in those gray areas. But like any A+ student, we must start with the hard and sometimes boring work of learning, knowing that we'll get to apply our knowledge later. It is incumbent upon us to understand the rules. Ignorance of laws is not an excuse in our legal system.

RULES IN CONTEXT

Rules don't exist in a vacuum; they interplay with the social contexts of their time and place. I saw this particularly after living in Europe and spending time in both Italy and Germany. While these two counties have (generally) the same laws and rules, they are polar opposites in how they follow those rules. In Germany, rules are sacrosanct and even the most minor rules are followed to the letter. In Italy, even the most critical rules are, as I heard repeatedly from our Italian friends, "just suggestions." You can see this in the traffic patterns when you walk or drive around Italy and Germany. In Germany, nobody ever jaywalks. Ever. I was once crossing a street in Germany with no cars to be seen in either direction, and I started to walk, and got an earful from a bunch of Germans. The rule was the rule, regardless.

Italy was entirely different, and it made for some truly terrifying driving experiences. A three-lane highway was always at least six lanes of cars. Drivers would miss their exits on the Autostrade *and then back up to take the exit.* Red lights were mere suggestions, and cars would come flying through regularly. Vespas would zip in and out of traffic, and we'd come upon a scooter fatality at least monthly on our drive home. Funny enough, though, even those rule-breaking ways had their limits. In Italy, if you saw a carabiniere (police officer) standing with a handheld sign, which they called a "lollipop," and they waved you over, everyone immediately complied . . . mostly because they knew there was authorization for the police to use their weapon if there was any hint of a lack of compliance.

Part of rule following is cultural, as laws are meant to represent how people approach rules overall. Part of it is incentive based. Different cultures set up different incentive (and disincentive) structures around rules, and obviously there are different consequences for breaking certain rules over others. A minor traffic violation doesn't carry the same consequences as stealing a car (unless you're in Italy and disregard the lollipop, I guess). Some rules carry such minor consequences for breaking them—both legally but also ethically and otherwise— that most of us break them routinely without even thinking. Weighing the costs and benefits of breaking those rules may be reasonable in some cases. I tried that in Germany when there were no cars coming and I didn't wait for the light at the crosswalk. Some situations may even call for breaking the rules for a greater good; those who hid Jews during the Holocaust were clearly breaking rules that should have been broken, even with dire consequences if discovered.

As a psychology student, I learned the cautionary tales of blind rule following. There wasn't a psychology class I can remember where we didn't talk about Stanley Milgram (the shock experiment) or Phil Zimbardo (the Stanford prison experiment) and the perils of following an authority figure unthinkingly and unquestioningly. I am not advocating for blind allegiance to authority figures or even blind allegiance to the rules, and the end of this chapter and particularly chapter 9 are dedicated to how we change the rules when they don't work anymore. And there are clearly rules and structures that don't work well, and some of those call for active resistance and upending the status quo. Some rules absolutely need to be broken to make society better. I am not discounting any of that in talking about how to play within the rules.

But in most cases, figuring out how to play the game and work within the rules will provide you with the most effective path to success. Even within the cases where a rule (or set of rules) needs to be changed, an understanding of the game and the current rules will help guide you in the best way to challenge or change the rules.

SCHOOLHOUSE ROCK FOR ADULTS

I could easily geek out on how our legal structure works—and I have, for most of my career. But here I'll give you just the basic structure you need to get started on your Unruly journey and point you to other places where you can take a deep dive if you want to join me in my geekiness.

I grew up in a politically active family, and there was very little that wasn't subject to debate in our house. So many people in my extended family went to law school (and particularly to the law school at the University of Michigan) that the former dean of Michigan Law called it blasphemy that I was a Wittenberg and chose to get a PhD instead of a JD. But even with all of that, I was shockingly clueless about how laws were made, interpreted, and changed—and particularly how much room there was to maneuver within the legal framework.

With apologies to my high school social studies teachers, all I really knew about how laws were made came from the *Schoolhouse Rock* of the 1970s on ABC.

When I found myself in a public policy role in the White House after walking away from academia, I still knew very little about how the government really worked. I'll leave it to *Schoolhouse Rock* to teach you how a bill gets passed through both houses of Congress and signed by the president. All of this is similar for state and local laws, but I'll talk here about federal rules to keep it as simple as possible.

But before we get into how rules are made, implemented, enforced, and interpreted, we need to quickly go back to high school government class and remember the concepts of tripartite government and separation of powers. We have three equal branches of government—the legislative branch that makes the laws, the executive branch that implements and enforces the laws, and the judicial branch that interprets the laws—and all of them serve as a check and balance on the others.

So, after a bill makes its way to becoming law, what next? Is that it? Does it just automatically become the new law, and everyone follows it exactly based on the language in the bill? The short answer is "not usually." Once bills are passed by Congress (legislative) and signed by the president (executive), they become law and are published in the United States Code (USC). You might hear this called "statutory law," since these laws come from a statute. Some bills are extremely short and give very little guidance about how they should be implemented. Some are detailed and "self-implementing," in that they are immediately in effect when passed. Some are mandatory to be implemented (and often give a specific timeline for implementation if they're not self-implementing), and some are permissive—they allow but don't require the executive branch agencies to set forth governing regulations.

Once a bill is signed into law, in most cases the next step is setting forth a regulation (also called a rule) to implement the law by the executive branch. This type of law is known as "administrative law." Once finalized, these regulations have the force of law, just like the bills signed into law by the president, and are published in the Code of Federal Regulations (CFR).

While regulations help to implement the laws, they are

often still fairly broad, and they won't answer every question of how things really work on the ground. That is often left to sub-regulatory documents like policy guidance, memos and circulars, and best-practice guidelines. These documents don't have the force of law, but they do help us determine what will be considered generally a safe harbor in interpreting the legal requirements in the USC and CFR language.

And then, because of the brilliance of our Founding Fathers, all of this—laws, regulations, sub-regulatory guidance—is subject to review by the judicial branch, which plays a crucial role as a check and balance on both the legislative and executive branches. The judges rule on specific cases and create precedent through case law.

All of this comes together to provide us with a legal structure that keeps lawyers gainfully employed because it is confusing, difficult to track and follow, and frequently changes. Those things that are truly settled are called "black-letter law"—that is the law you probably don't have much room for interpretation within. But most law is not truly black-letter law; it is not entirely settled and still has some significant room for interpretation.

GET TO GROUND TRUTH

So much of what we "know" comes from secondhand or thirdhand sources. People rarely go back to the source documentation to check what they're being told. It has gotten so much worse over the course of my lifetime; now we are fed a curated set of information through social media. Opinions masquerade as facts, and falsehoods aren't challenged. With the algorithms, our "facts" become more and more unbalanced, so that we are seeing something entirely different than our neighbor down the street or someone across town. It is imperative that we get to the "ground truth" of actual facts, rather than taking what we hear and read and consume at face value.

Years ago, I taught statistics classes. One of my favorite assignments was to have my students find a splashy, exciting research study discussed in the popular press and compare the findings as they were relayed in the press with the findings in the research paper, the actual source document. Going back to the source document for any subject is always illuminating. A popular press article is looking for sensationalism to get the attention of readers and must boil things down to one quick and easily digestible takeaway. The research findings are almost always more nuanced when you go back to the source document. This is why scientific research can often give the feeling of whiplash; the popular press will report one study that they say "proves" hormone replacement therapy (HRT) is terrible for women and should never be given, then another or later report takes the position that HRT is a lifesaver that all women should use. The truth is much more nuanced, but the reporting isn't, and also doesn't take into account any of the other studies in scientific literature to provide context.

I often lament our headline culture that drives nuance out of so much of our lives. It was bad enough almost thirty years ago when I was in graduate school and would first ask my students to do this assignment. Now, with our news coming from social media in bite-sized snippets with absolutely no nuance, and very little in the way of filtering for truth or credibility, it is so much worse. Combatting headline culture—not just in news but across all aspects, including the written rules and policies that govern our lives—takes the work of going back to the source documentation to get to the ground truth. But where do we find all these sources of ground truth, particularly as it relates to laws and regulations and policy?

The rules start with the federal (and state and local) laws, regulations, and guidelines, but depending on what you're trying to do, they may include corporate policies and handbooks, industry-specific certification requirements and best practices or safe harbors, or academic or industry research. Each case will require a deep dive to find an exhaustive review of anything that could drive required compliance. I'll run through a quick overview of how you can get to the federal laws and rules. The same tools will apply, generally, to any deep dive you do at the industry or corporate level.

Finding the federal laws and regulations is, at least on the surface, fairly easy—you can get all of the US Code and Code of Federal Regulations online. I've found that law.cornell.edu is a trustworthy and up-to-date reference and is intuitive to navigate. If you have an entry point—you know specifically which law or regulation applies—you can start there. But you can get to that entry point any number of other ways—from a simple Google search to a review of what experts have written. If you're starting with something like a corporate handbook, reading the entire document or word searching it for specific mentions or using the index may be the easiest starting point. Usually, laws or regulations make reference to other related laws or regulations, and it is important you follow that first law or rule to the related others. This is one reason I love the

Cornell site; it has hyperlinks to related citations. If you stop at the first reference and don't continue to the other references, you risk missing critical pieces. I generally locate the first reference I can and follow every cross-citation that is listed within it, and then I start again and do some additional searching for an initial entry point and follow it through. The process must be iterative to be effective.

I know that this can be overwhelming, but once you get comfortable tracking through the citations, it gets much more comfortable. I generally keep a Word document open to take notes of what I'm finding, because it can get confusing to track all the cross-citations. You don't have to get a perfect understanding up front—just get a listing of what citations you think may be applicable and try to get a gestalt understanding of the lay of the land. In some instances, you can and should go beyond just the law and regulation language; deeper dives can take you to additional policies or best practices or guidance documentation. You can also look to judicial or administrative case law.

When I'm getting into a new realm, I will generally take an initial deep dive into the laws and rules and guidance documents just to get my feet solidly underneath me. And yes, I recognize that it makes me a total geek. But the real magic comes when you're trying to figure out if there's wiggle room somewhere to do something very specific. That's when acting like a detective gets fun. If you have an idea of how you might do something differently, start with one citation like we discussed above, and follow the trail all the way down the rabbit hole to ask if there's anything you can find that would preclude you from doing what you want. This way, you're not just deep

diving into the rules for a broad-based understanding, which is
sleep inducing even for the geekiest among us. You're starting
to get Unruly and asking very specific questions of the rules
and laws and seeing if you have any barriers in the rules. You're
going back to the source documents to get to the ground truth
of what is allowed and precluded.

TWO PEOPLE, THREE OPINIONS

After finding the ground truth, we need to interpret what it
means. Approaching legal language can be intimidating for
those of us who didn't go to law school—with all the "shalls"
and "mays" and other legalese. That said, it is absolutely possible for non-lawyers to get a solid understanding of the rules
without relying on high-priced lawyers, particularly in situations that aren't high stakes (where noncompliance can lead
to serious consequences). All of us will have different tolerance
for what we can do without help, but as you get more expertise
in your field, you'll find that you have much more comfort
because you've seen generally how similar rules get interpreted
across situations. Even in those cases where you need to engage legal counsel, your own review and initial interpretation
is helpful to be able to formulate the right questions, which
may help to keep your legal bills in line and allow the lawyer to
understand and evaluate your unique approach.

Regardless of if you attempt this on your own or with legal assistance, this is where thinking like a detective comes
in handy. People can have entirely different interpretations
of the same language, and many of those can be reasonable

interpretations. I saw this early on, just after I left the White House and was working on the base in Italy. One of the Navy employees was trying to interpret a rule that had recently been published that impacted the operations on base, and he had a very specific interpretation. He told me that *obviously* the person who drafted the rule meant X, and I just didn't understand the way rules were written if I thought any differently. But funny enough, it was language that I had written when I was in the White House the year before, and it never even dawned on me that it could be interpreted the way he was thinking. I thought I had drafted it clearly—and I still think he was wrong in reading into it the way he did—but it was a good lesson that language can be interpreted multiple different ways.

You will find yourself down a rabbit hole very quickly, trust me, but if you can make sense of all of it, you can get somewhere useful. I usually take a first run-through of the rules and laws to see if I can get a general feel for what they're saying, and then a basic matrix for which citations are cross-referencing, so that I know I have a full picture of what governs the situation. But on the second read, I start asking questions (I list some of those below, as a starting point) in my mind about how it might be interpreted differently. Your first task will be to find those differing interpretations in your Unruly quest before next determining which interpretation makes the most sense to you and gets you to where you want to be.

Of note, our laws are often in conflict with each other—so sometimes you will find one place that seems to suggest you can't do something, where another says you should do that same thing. It can get very confusing and frustrating, particularly when you're trying to do the right thing and follow the rules. And interpretation of rules is an art rather than a science. That's why we can easily have two people and three (or even more) opinions. Most rules are written specifically to allow for interpretation and wiggle room, which can be wonderful and allow for innovation, but it can make for some serious heartburn as well.

In those cases, if I can find a clear path that allows me to do what I want, and I don't see something specifically prohibiting me from doing it, I'll document my thinking and move forward. If one interpretation makes sense and gets me to where I want to be, I may be able to take that route even if there's another interpretation that other people hold that would preclude the action. We'll talk about optionality later in the book, but in interpreting rules and finding a clear path to get to each different option we want on the table, we preserve our optionality effectively.

So, what questions should you start asking of the rules in that second pass through your review (with the first run through being the first review of all the rules themselves)?

- What do the rules *require* me to do? (Look for language like "shall" or "must" here.)
- What do the rules *permit* me to do? (Look for language like "may" here.)
- What do the rules *prohibit* me from doing? (Look for language like "shall not" or "must not" here.)
- Do the rules speak at all to what I'm thinking about doing? Are they permissive or prohibitive or just silent?
- Are there any rules in conflict with other rules? Where are they? What does the preponderance of the rules seem to say? Where does the conflict arise?

- What about guidance documents or case law? Does it get any more specific about what is required, permitted, or prohibited? Or do they remain silent?
- If the documents seem to prohibit what I want to do, are they legal language or just guidance? Is there a mechanism to obtain a waiver from the prohibition?
- What was the legislative or regulatory intent of the law? On a plain reading, does it seem to allow for what I want to do? Does what I want to do seem to fit within the spirit of the law as well as the letter of the law?
- If the laws or rules prohibit what I want to do, is there another creative solution that might get me to the outcome I want? If so, run through the above list of questions again to see if that path would be allowed.

I've found that law firms often put out public-facing reviews of law changes or relevant laws that their clients—or, in this case, potential clients—may struggle with. Search for those—either by flagging law firm citations in your original search or conducting a targeted search for "law firm" and "opinion" around your topic and use them as a starting point. They might answer all or most of your questions, or they may point you to someone who can help quickly and efficiently answer the additional questions you have.

ADVOCACY AS AN ART FORM

Laws, policies, and interpretations aren't static. They morph near constantly—a book of laws was no sooner published than it was out of date before the advent of the internet. That makes it exhausting to keep up with the law—and keeps lawyers in business forever. But that constant change allows for effective advocacy to update laws that don't work well. And sometimes, to get Unruly, we need to advocate for modifications to the laws to allow for new options for getting to the best outcome. Sometimes, the rules *do* preclude us from doing something that makes sense, and there's no good reason for those rules to be in place. To do what we want, sometimes we need to be the ones to change the rules. We'll get further into broader advocacy in part 3, but let's talk briefly here about how to make alterations when rules get in the way of doing what you know is right in your own Unruly journey.

Advocacy is, at its base, a way of influencing any of the branches of government in how rules are established, interpreted, or changed. Depending on which parts you're trying to influence, you can approach the executive, legislative, or judicial branches to do so. There are very clear ways of approaching each branch of government, but in every case, we can get creative in how we do so.

For example, when you have what you believe is a solid interpretation of a rule that differs from the standard interpretation, and the executive branch agency doesn't seem to agree with it, I've found that's a time when separation of powers works to your advantage. Leverage your elected officials on the legislative side to ask questions for you. Their constituent services team can be an effective resource; when a congressional representative (or a state representative, or a county commissioner, or whatever level makes sense for the issue at hand) asks a question, the issue generally gets noticed. It doesn't always mean it will go in your favor, but it can be useful.

Beyond the formal advocacy channels within the government, a ton of advocacy is just changing hearts and minds. A lot of government rule changes happen because the zeitgeist changes and the lawmakers and agencies eventually catch up with it. My favorite example of one of the best advocates I've ever known is Ashley. She found herself in a very gray area after rules were changed within the military. Don't Ask/Don't Tell (DADT) had been repealed, and for the first time she was able to be open about her marriage to her wife, who was an active-duty soldier. Previously, she had to pretend she was the nanny for her own kids. They were at Fort Bragg (now Fort Liberty), and Ashley went to join the spouse group that supported families. These groups are particularly helpful during the deployments that were happening so often back then. The processes had not caught up with the updated rules, and Ashley did not yet have a dependent ID card, although the legal change made it official that she could be formally recognized as a spouse. However, the family group independently would not allow her to join.

She did two things to make her case; the first was to advocate to the military officer in charge and get some recognition in the media for the situation, which drove pressure that allowed her to join the group. But the second, and I think the more critical piece, was to try to find common ground with them. Although she did successfully drive a policy change through her formal advocacy, she didn't demand that the spouses themselves change their minds. What she did, instead, was approach them and talk about what they had in common, which was being the spouse of a deployed soldier. She appealed to their common humanity around the updates the group would get from the Army about their deployed soldier-spouses. When Ashley was not included in the group, she and her kids were not privy to those updates and that support. No matter what people thought about LGBT issues, they could relate to the challenges that a spouse at home with kids experiences during a deployment.

I saw this work in a way that absolutely astounded me. These spouses took that one small step toward understanding where Ashley was coming from, and then one step became two, and three, and four. In short order, I watched some of the loudest detractors of the repeal of DADT become the strongest advocates in support of the LGBT community within the military—because Ashley humanized her challenges and aligned them with the similar trials they all faced. She didn't demand anything beyond that they talk to her, face to face, human to human, and try to find that understanding.

I think that went a long way in "normalizing" the inclusion of same-gender spouses into the spouse groups, and fairly quickly it became a big nothing burger. Nothing to see here, just a standard spouse group. That's not to say that every advocacy issue should start with marginal changes and meeting people where they are. But Ashley's impressive and continued advocacy in one-on-one conversations made a massive difference in the way huge swaths of people approached her and other LGBT military families.

I know rules can feel boring and limiting, but truly understanding the rules is the first piece and can be freeing as it builds confidence, sets appropriate boundaries, and facilitates effective wayfinding.

THE INVISIBLE RULE BOOK

I am not one for games of chance, which is kind of funny now that my company was bought by the tribe that owns one of the largest resort casino in North America. But let's use card games to understand our next step in our Unruly journey. Most card games—take blackjack as an example—have pretty easy, straightforward written rules. In blackjack, everyone is dealt two cards (one face up, another face down) and then each player can request additional cards face up. Whoever gets closest to a combined total of twenty-one without going over wins. But there are layers on top of the basic rules that will help players win more frequently. There are the norms—if your cards total seventeen or more, don't ask for another card (or "hit"); and then there are deeper strategies that the best card players use, often based on what cards are showing for the dealer and others at the table. While blackjack has components of luck, skill can help tremendously if you know those unwritten strategies—the invisible rule book—beyond just the basic rules.

Similarly, we can layer additional guidelines, norms, and expectations on top of the structured and written rules and policies that we talked about in chapter 1 that are enforced at the corporate and governmental levels. Think about it this way: Following the written rules can keep you from getting in trouble. Understanding the invisible rule book can get you to baseline success. And these two layers of the rules are critical to master before you can really get Unruly, which can take you to true breakout success.

Too often, I hear from aspiring business owners that they're doing everything right and still not getting anywhere—not even to baseline success. Almost always, I find that they're playing the surface-level game by the written rules, but they don't understand the way the game is really played using the unwritten rules, and that is what is holding them back. When I first started out in GovCon, I was told that you find a request for a proposal, write a strong proposal that follows exactly what they ask for (in other words, complies with the written rules), and the best proposal wins. While on the surface the advice is correct, and all contracts (generally) follow that RFP to compliant proposal-to-award model, there is *so* much nuance underlying that generic set of rules. In reality, you could write the absolute perfect proposal and never ever win any contracts this way, no matter how qualified you are to perform the work. I can't tell you how many people spend way too much time and effort following that formula without ever realizing that there is an entirely different set of rules that are critical for even baseline success in the industry.

The challenge in these unwritten rules is exactly that: They are unwritten. It is much harder to find out how the "game" really works, especially when you are on the outside trying to break into an industry or when you change career tracks. To understand how the game really gets played you must go beyond the written rules. This chapter takes on the challenge of how you can uncover and gain understanding about these unwritten rules found in the invisible rule book.

FINDING AND UNDERSTANDING THE UNWRITTEN RULES

Learning the written rules is mostly about legwork; you need to know where to look to find the rules, and then you need to interpret those rules (or find the already-existing interpretations of those rules). Because the law is, by definition, written down, it is available for all to review and interpret. Once you know where to find the rules and how to interpret them, you can do that without any outside help if you so desire. The more you work to interpret rules, the better you will get as the language and structure of laws and other written rules become more familiar. You can work through written rules without ever having to speak directly to another human being, but you need a different approach once you move to the unwritten rules where the game has less clarity.

With unwritten rules, the experience and demands are entirely the opposite of written rules. There is generally nowhere to find those unwritten rules without interacting in some way with those who are succeeding in that world. I've found that, hands down, the best way to do it is to surround yourself with others who know the specific game that you're trying to play.

It is critical to note that "the game" is played differently depending on the industry or even your subsector of the industry. It often comes with a type of shorthand that can reveal your depth of comfort and knowledge. And, while you might be a recognized expert in your current industry, the moment you pivot to a different market space, you'll quickly come up against those unwritten rules that can stop you in your tracks until you learn how things really get done.

I saw this repeatedly with transitioning military service members—particularly active duty who were retiring after a full career and were pivoting to a civilian career. Ironically, those who had been the most successful in the military often had the hardest time learning the invisible rule book of the civilian world. They knew how to navigate the military career ladder: what to say and not to say when jockeying for a new position, how to position themselves for the career progression they wanted, how to work effectively within the military bureaucracy. They had figured out the unwritten military rule book throughout their long and successful military career. But unless they realized quickly that there were entirely different norms and expectations in their post-uniform world, they would fall flat on their face for the first time in decades, because the unwritten rules are much different in nonmilitary industries (even those closely affiliated with the military, surprisingly). About half of newly separated veterans leave their first post-military job within a year, with another 15 percent leaving within two years, and I've seen that most of their missteps come from simply missing the unwritten rules of the new game in their new world. Too many amplify what *they* think they bring to the new organization, without giving enough attention to what the new organization needs from their position and their expertise and without absorbing and assimilating to the unwritten ways and a whole new environment.

People can and should become your greatest teachers, guides, and waymakers when immersing yourself in these unwritten areas. There are multiple ways to access the expertise, but you need to be proactive and intentional about seeking this information. Those who can offer guidance range from the closest to the most impersonal relationships, but engaging in the unwritten rules generally requires at least some interaction with people to become proficient and agile. You will likely tap into all types of relationships along this spectrum as you first access, then learn the nuances of, and finally deeply immerse yourself in the gray areas to get a full understanding. The combination of the understanding of the written and unwritten rules—getting up to speed in your industry—is the necessary precursor to becoming Unruly, but also the baseline for even standard success. Without understanding both levels, you will find yourself believing you're doing everything right while continuously spinning your wheels.

Monique followed a path that exemplifies how to leverage all the different components of learning the unwritten rules. She was one of six kids growing up housing insecure. She attended a community college at seventeen but found herself unexpectedly pregnant at twenty. She quickly married and transferred to her new husband's college, but after two years they couldn't afford for her to continue. She applied for scholarships and was able to get one of the original Gates Millennium scholarships at twenty-two, which paid for the completion of her college degree and her master's degree and provided some leadership training and other support and guidance. Her husband was injured in a deployment while she was in the program. In managing two kids and a husband with significant war-induced challenges, she joined a support group on base run by a wonderful woman, Patty, who eventually helped her get a job with the Military Officers Association of America (MOAA). (Patty herself parlayed her decades of volunteer and paid experience in the military family space, years later, into a political appointment as the deputy assistant secretary of defense for military community and family policy, in true Unruly fashion.) Monique's position gave her entrance into a broad support network of military family advocates, and eventually other nonprofit and corporate executives who championed her throughout her career. She moved up through the ranks from development associate to executive director of high-impact, well-regarded philanthropic organizations, and she eventually became a VP for one of the top nonprofit consulting firms in the nation.

Monique had a start in life that could have easily held her back from breakout success, but at each turn she leveraged both her close relationships and the arm's-length experts that were available to her throughout her career. While the educational opportunities were important, starting with the access she had from the Gates fellowship, those relationships were key in teaching her how the game is truly played, and how to open the doors to opportunities to get in the game in the first place. Just like for Monique, from the closest to the most impersonal relationships, *people* will be your key to understanding the unwritten rules of the game. Let's look at these relationships and how they can help guide you in grasping the unwritten rules.

We will start from the arm's-length relationships to the closest advisors.

ACCESS THE ARM'S-LENGTH EXPERTS

The most arm's-length options for learning the unwritten rules are courses—targeted to the way the game is really played, rather than the surface-level written rules—where experts provide lectures or interactive discussions. For Monique, this was what the leadership courses provided by the Gates program offered.

WWC was founded well before webinars, podcasts, or many other present-day ways to get information out there came into vogue. But when we were starting out, our leadership team found a whole lot of great information through very targeted classes that we took. We happened upon a series of classes that were not inexpensive, but they were taught by the absolute experts, and they went through not only the written rules but the norms and expectations in the industry. We got lucky in finding the first one, and then continued to take every class they provided on the topics we needed more information about. We found other courses that were less helpful, and even when they were less expensive (or free), we avoided those going forward because they weren't worth the time investment.

The key to finding the ones that could help you comprehend the "real" game was to locate those that weren't just regurgitating laws and regulations. You can often tell just by the descriptions if these courses are at least somewhat likely to tackle the unwritten rules. There is certainly a place for the dry "here are the written rules and their interpretation" courses as well, and those will talk about compliance, new legal interpretations, and step-by-step guides. For the unwritten rules, you may see things like "the unofficial guide" or "breaking in" or "how to *really* do X." You can also look to see who is putting it on; oftentimes, the more formal industry organizations or government entities will be doing the compliance-type courses, while independent organizations will give the insiders' view on unwritten rules. You can usually tell a lot by simply the irreverence versus formality of the course descriptions.

Critically, once we found a good class with good instructors, we then often cultivated relationships with the instructors so that we could ask them what the norms were and whether there were places we could push on those norms. We figured out a way to make even these mostly arm's-length interactions more personal, when so many of our classmates didn't.

Beyond the classes and the conferences that were, twenty years ago, already hard to sort through to find the best value options, now you've got podcasts, and webinars, and talks and presentations, and mastery-level classes and guided-mentoring groups, and retreats, and virtual retreats, and all manner of other options for gathering information about how the game is really played. At this point, the information that is out there can be entirely overwhelming. There is so much information available that you need some keys to curate it so that you can find the most effective experts who really have some differentiated information to offer. The best way to find those great courses is to ask around and see if anyone recommends any specific options, or test out a few and curate them as you find the value (or lack thereof) within them. You won't always get it right in what you pick, and that's okay. When something doesn't work, *stop participating.* Even once you've invested time and treasure, it is okay to move on. Stop reading a book instead of forcing yourself to finish it (hopefully not this book!), turn off the webinar, don't go back to the class after lunch.

MANDATORY FUN (AKA NETWORKING)

Beyond the online and in-person courses, another layer to the relationships are industry-specific networking events that generally bridge information sharing through speakers or panels that offer in-person networking with others in your industry. I learned a ton, particularly in our early days, at large GovCon conferences, or regularly scheduled networking meetings that are industry specific (such as breakfasts, lunches, happy hours), or groups that are more broad-based (peer-to-peer "mastermind" groups, affinity groups that cut across industries—the list of options is almost endless). Networking groups can be a small investment in time and money and at least get you pointed in the right direction. Conferences can be more expensive—in terms of fees and travel expenses, and also, critically, your time—so you need to pick and choose those carefully to determine which ones are of use. Ask around, try a few of the networking breakfasts/coffees/lunches, test out a conference or two to start. But again, start curating and culling these opportunities early and often if they don't bring value. These events have a dual purpose in your understanding of the unwritten rules: first, they give valuable information on how the game is really played because there are real live experts who you can interact with and ask meaningful questions of, but also, they can serve as a place to grow your close network that we'll talk about later in the chapter.

You could easily spend all your time at conferences and none of your time doing your "real" job if you're not careful. The same goes for the classes and the online training—they can be helpful, but they need to be balanced with actually *doing* your job. I've seen way too many people think that networking was the way to success—and it certainly is a critical component, but at some point, you must stop learning and just start doing. You will *never* have perfect information, and you will *never* know everything you're supposed to know, and you'll need to get comfortable in the discomfort. (We'll talk a lot more about this in the next chapter when we talk about imposter syndrome.) You absolutely need to learn continuously, but you have to continuously *do* as well. Even from your earliest days in a new industry, you must take the leap and balance your *learning* with *doing*—try to land a sale, try to build the prototype, whatever the *doing* step is, you've got to move forward on it.

You might get nothing out of the doing but a good learning experience. But you can't let the fact that you don't know everything stop you from starting. You will make mistakes—we all make them even once we've become experts—but you can't let the fear of not getting it perfect handcuff you, or you're just engaging in a vanity project. It can easily be a crutch to feel like you're doing something by networking, and it can feel good and productive, but networking and learning alone won't get you to the success you want. We will talk a lot more about this in part 2.

MASTERING THE STANDARD PLAYBOOK

Just before the firm got our first contract, I ended up teaching a good portion of the MBA program on the Navy base in Italy, even though I didn't have an MBA or anything close to it, and I had never worked in business. Education can be very useful—which is why one of the critical things that the Gates program did for Monique was to pay for her college and graduate school. There are lots of things in business that are just pretty standard, and you absolutely should learn the way that most people gain success, so you don't reinvent the wheel when you don't have to. Compliance in pretty much every realm is standardized and something you don't want to mess with. Accounting—that's something you don't want to reinvent. Even for some of the noncritical functions, it is totally fine to just do what others do and not hassle with it. If there are a couple of standard HR systems or accounting software platforms, pick the one that works best for you, but you don't need to throw them all out and create your own for everything you do.

In the firm, we called these standard operations the "MBA playbook," even though some of it likely comes from sources other than a traditional business education—you could just as easily call it the "public policy playbook" or the "legal play-book," if that applies. For ease, I'll call it the "standard play-book" throughout the rest of the book. I'll talk a lot in the next part about throwing out the standard playbook when it makes sense, but first you need to figure out the rules behind the standard playbook, why they exist, and when it makes sense to follow them and when it makes sense to throw them out. On balance, you should probably use the vast majority of what everyone else does, especially concerning those things where there is no benefit in doing something differently. It is crucial, though, to figure out which operational pieces of the standard playbook are stopping you from differentiating yourself.

And there are all sorts of ways to learn the standard playbook—from the large open-source subscription courses to stand-alone courses to actual MBA programs—and you can also hire the experts who do know each of these areas and bring them into your leadership team, your support network (which we'll discuss below), or outsource to them. But you still must know enough to oversee what they're doing and challenge the assumptions that they make simply because it is "how everyone does things." This is especially true with those things that may be considered "best practices." They can easily become outdated or lack application to your particular operation.

One of my most effective ways of learning the unwritten standard playbook was to go on a listening tour of people in my industry who had faced a specific issue before me. I'd informally interview them about the issues they'd encountered at that point and how they handled them. Critically, I didn't take everything they said at face value. I did this particularly as we were facing a specific turning point in our firm's trajectory, something colloquially known in our industry as "the Valley of Death." When a firm is coming out of small business status, it graduates to "full-and-open" competition with no built-in transition period. Even within the most successful firms that make it to small business "graduation," over 97 percent don't make it as a viable non-small business. I talked to probably three to four dozen leaders of firms who had either made the transition well, had made the transition well but then failed later, or had struggled with the transition at other points for various reasons.

These open discussions provided me with an honest picture of what had gone well and what hadn't. Some of the information from the other leaders was self-serving, to be sure, but in gathering *all* the data from so many sources, I could get a picture of what worked across the board and what didn't. And then, critically, just like the rest of the standard playbook, I was able to modify the few things within that playbook to be what would work best *for us* and allow us to differentiate ourselves and stay true to what built us. From that set of meetings, we developed a Valley of Death strategic plan, and we were able to meet every strategic marker on that plan earlier than expected at higher metrics than I had set. But most of that wouldn't have been obvious to me unless I had sat down with everyone, asked the hard questions, and gotten honest answers.

CURATING CONNECTIONS

One of the most common questions I get when I'm speaking or mentoring is: "What is your most important piece of advice?" I consistently answer: **Find your village**. Surround yourself with people who love and support you unconditionally, who truly celebrate your success and will get down in the mud with you when you're falling apart. More than any other factor, my unconditionally supportive village is the secret to my success, both professionally and personally. Sure, it takes hard work and smarts and all the other tools that we will talk about in this book, but if you strip all of that away and are just left with a strong and supportive village, your life will be pretty remarkable regardless. And portions of your village can be your best way to find out the unwritten rules and how to apply them to your specific situation.

You may not make friends easily or enjoy the process. Your village can be effective regardless of whether it is large or small, depending on how you cultivate your relationships. I've seen people thrive with a small, tight-knit village, and others flail with what looks from the outside like a large and robust one that isn't truly supportive. The key is to cultivate the village that is right for you, provides you with the support you need, and can grow with you as your life circumstances change.

While "village" is an all-encompassing term for everyone around that supports you in some way, there are two components of your village that are specifically critical in learning the unwritten rules and navigating the overall ups and downs in your life. Those critical subsets of your village are your **kitchen cabinet** and your **concentric circles**. When we look at the trajectory of Monique's career, it was her support network that helped her navigate the professional (and personal) challenges and set her on an Unruly path to breakout success. Without those key relationships, she still would have met a baseline of success in whatever field she chose just based on her hard work and educational success, but her substantial leaps would have been impossible.

UNCONDITIONAL SUPPORT IS KEY

Before we get into the ways that you can leverage your kitchen cabinet and concentric circles to learn the unwritten rules, it is critical that you take those people from a strong and supportive village, first and foremost. Your village should be made up of those close friends, family, and professional contacts who play a critical role as your cheer squad, your emotional support, your day-to-day get-through-life folks, your trusted advisors. They bring their wisdom, you share a moral compass with them, and they are implicitly trustworthy to you. You will be pulling from your village for both your kitchen cabinet and your concentric circles of support.

There's nothing more important than making sure these folks in your life are giving and strong and available. If you find yourself in toxic relationships in this group, it will impact everything else you try to do. Obviously, everyone has bad days or even difficult weeks or months, and relationships certainly will have their ups and downs as well, but relationships that aren't bringing positive energy on balance mean it is time to cull this group to those who do. There is no amount of effort on your part that can overcome the dragging effect if your inner circle of friends and family continues to pull you down. That's not to say that your origins determine your ongoing destiny—you can absolutely break free from toxic relationships and thrive—but you can't do it unless you take action to set up barriers or boundaries and limit access or opportunities where they have the opportunity to pull you down. They should be your hype squad, your get-down-in-the-muck-with-you crew, your ride or dies.

It is important to note that there may end up being plenty of people you interact with who you don't implicitly trust but must stay part of your life for any number of reasons. You can, and likely must, still have relationships with them, and they may never know that they're not part of your village, but those people should be held at an emotional distance. They can play some necessary roles, but if they don't fit the standard for unconditional support, they shouldn't sit in a place where they could steal any of your peace.

Supporting you unconditionally doesn't mean that these people always agree with you. In fact, some of the best support can come from someone challenging the way you look at an issue. But that challenge comes from wanting to see you succeed, not trying to undercut you. My village members routinely give me tough love when I'm being silly, and I do the same for them. As one of my close friends says, "Tough love is my love language." You should know that your close friends love you when they're willing to effectively challenge you rather than just blindly cheer you on.

I was recently talking to a member of my village, and she noted that one of the most critical drivers of these close relationships is shared vulnerability. It is a bit of a chicken-and-egg thing to be comfortable in being vulnerable, because you must take the leap to be vulnerable to get to that deep relationship, but when you get a signal that you can trust someone—when they're potentially going to lift you to being your best self—sharing your vulnerable inner thoughts is what creates that strong intimacy. You certainly don't start out revealing your vulnerabilities to someone you just met—well, unless you're a military spouse in a new area, and you need someone to watch your toddler when you go into early labor, as this friend did the night I met her—but making yourself open and vulnerable is the way to drive these strong villages. Sure, sometimes someone will turn out to be unworthy of your trust, but even with that disappointment, you've come out on top, because others will be worth it, and you wouldn't have found them without taking a chance on deeper friendships.

This vulnerability—this deep connection—is the exact opposite of a **transactional relationship**. Transactional relationships "keep score" and make sure that everyone stays equal. Deep relationships have no scorecard. I am a big believer that the energy you circulate in the world—not the "woo-woo" kind of energy, but the positive stuff you put out there—ends up coming back to you exponentially. There is something critical about doing good just to do good, *not* to get anything back, that ironically makes it come back around. Transactional begets transactional, and bad behavior begets alienation from good people.

Adam Grant talks a lot about this in his book *Give and Take,* which is one of my absolute favorite books because it captures, with actual research, how I've approached all my adult relationships. When you have deep relationships, those people have seen you in the mud and the muck of the worst times of your life and have been there to help you out of it. When they've been around for that, they're genuinely excited to see your wins—without jealousy, without reservation—because they also know that you'll be there in the muck with them, and you'll reach behind and pull them up when they need it.

Your Kitchen Cabinet

A critical component of your village for professional purposes will be your kitchen cabinet. While they can guide you in learning the specific unwritten rules in your industry or the broader professional context, they do far more than that. Just like the US president's cabinet of advisors, these are your own personal advisors, but instead of sitting around the conference table in the Roosevelt Room in the White House, they're sitting around your (usually virtual) kitchen table. These are the people who have the specific professional skills that you'll end up needing as you navigate and try to understand these unwritten rules.

This should be a fairly small group, your inner sanctum of close advisors. I'm not sure there's a specific optimal size for your kitchen cabinet, and the members certainly can and will change over time. People can play multiple roles and likely will. But, at bare minimum, in your kitchen cabinet, I think you need:

- **The cheerleader:** This is the one who props you up when you're feeling overwhelmed, or when you start suffering from imposter syndrome. They are your hype squad and will remind you of just how amazing you are.
- **The naysayer:** This is the pessimist who can find every single risk you may face, but critically, they're also the one who can help you come up with risk mitigation strategies to get you over the barrier.
- **The enforcer:** This is the one who gives you the tough

love you need and keeps you honest about if you're do-ing what you set out to do. They're the one who will have the tough conversations with you and not let you get away with excuses. Honestly, for me, most of my kitchen cabinet can and does play this role.

- **The wise one**: This is the traditional mentor, often but not always the older and more experienced person, who has been there and done that, and can give you ad-vice from a position where they've seen and done most of what you're trying to do. In military circles, we use the term "gray beard," but these folks can certainly be women and don't necessarily have to be older to play this role.

- **The peer**: This is the one slogging through it with you in the trenches. They are facing the same basic things at the same time and can be your support and your real-ity testing. They also often have the best resources that they've found recently for the same practical issues.

In addition to these roles, you want at least one person in your kitchen cabinet who is in your industry and therefore knows the unwritten rules (and, as you're learning a new industry, probably more than one), and one that has absolutely no idea about your industry and therefore can ask the novice questions that can break you out of the standard playbook and get to the heart of the Unruly approach. Cabinet members don't have to individually know all the rules in your specific industry, and often they can bring perspective to ask those Unruly questions when they're not directly involved, as long as you have at least one or two other members that are in the industry to give you the baseline norms and expectations. Diversity in your kitchen cabinet will safeguard you against the groupthink that creates echo chambers, where everyone has the same blind spots. In my kitchen cabinet, I have men and women, a diversity of races and ethnicities, Democrats and Republicans and independents, and wide age spans. I also have people from all phases of my life.

I don't hold cabinet meetings—although I've seen a formal board of advisors, even a personal one rather than a corporate one, be effective in some situations—and some of my cabinet have never met the others in the cabinet. I will sometimes bring a few of my cabinet members together, either for an actual in-person meeting or a text thread or a Zoom meeting, to solve a specific issue where each of their perspectives, while valuable individually, become even more powerful by engaging the hive mind. As you try to get Unruly in your industry, this hive mind is critical to help you get outside of the day-to-day and ask the Unruly questions with both an understanding of the current norms and an ability to push outside those norms. They can help guide where those trip wires might be and how to manage around them if you want to push the boundaries.

Your Concentric Circles of Support

Beyond your kitchen cabinet, I think about concentric circles of support. These are the supportive folks who won't be in your kitchen cabinet for various reasons. They know and support you, but you'll more rarely tap them for assistance. No matter where they fall in your concentric circles, these relationships need to be maintained and cultivated. And that cultivation can't be—and certainly can't feel—transactional. Even in the wider circles, these relationships must be genuine and meaningful, even if they're not nearly as deep as the relationships in your inner sanctum.

Not everyone that you have a relationship with can or should be part of your kitchen cabinet, or even part of your concentric circles. They should be a curated group, even if the group is fairly large. You have to trust them, and particularly trust that they have your interests at heart. So, it isn't how often you interact with or work with people that defines this group as one of your trusted circles. It is how effectively you can mutually support each other and how genuine they are. And people can come in and out of those positions of trust. I don't burn bridges except in extreme circumstances. I just understand when a relationship becomes transactional, and I don't continue to count these people in my village.

I can't even count how many people are in my concentric circles. I am not a collector of things—I despise knickknacks and clutter—but I *am* a collector of people. I am still in touch with my favorite high school teachers, my old graduate school professor, and my favorite boss from my White House days, all of whom have jumped in to help me with recent projects without hesitation; plus my old forensics coach and her husband who helped me with my TEDx script when I had a panic attack over having committed to it.

I have also learned to have no fear in approaching new people and cultivating relationships with them, because that has been my best way of bringing in newer kitchen cabinet members or members of my broader concentric circles. Even now, it doesn't come easily to me—although it has become much easier through practice—but I force myself to approach new people and show my vulnerability. And while not everyone has become a member of my village after approaching them, I've yet to have any horribly negative response to the approach.

On the topic of finding mentors, please *do not* ask someone to be your mentor. I have never once gotten a mentor by asking them to be my mentor, and most of the people I call mentors wouldn't classify themselves that way. Mentors must be cultivated over time and with effort.

Recently, I spoke at a wonderful veterans' conference and talked with some remarkable veteran business owners. And I had at least a dozen people come to me, introduce themselves, and *immediately* ask me to mentor them. Mentoring, done right, is a *huge* commitment, and a long-standing and deep relationship. When you first meet someone that you may want to be your mentor, ask them for five minutes of their time, or maybe ask them if you can take them for a coffee (and don't be surprised if they say no). Ask for a quick phone call. Start small and respect their time. Come to that first meeting knowing who they are and ask them specific, targeted questions about an issue you are facing that you think they may have conquered based on their history. Unless they are a career coach and you're willing to pay for their time, do not immediately ask them to be your mentor.

I'll give you an example of two business owners who both attempted to enter mentoring relationships with me around the same time, both through close and trusted connections of mine, with very different results.

The first one showed up late, didn't know anything about me or my company, and within minutes of our greeting, flat-out asked me what I could do for him. Out of respect for the concentric circle member who asked me to talk to him, I gave him an hour of my time regardless, and I provided as much guidance as I could within that time. He called me a few weeks later, not to thank me, but to tell me that my advice was "actually" surprisingly useful and that he was going to make me his mentor. He continued to try to demand time and became very vocal when he didn't get what he expected out of me—my time, but also introductions and contract positions as a handout. Needless to say, he doesn't get any more of my time or access to my network.

That same week, I had breakfast with another business owner. He came, notebook in hand, and started by thanking me for taking my time to talk to him. He had done his homework and came to the meeting with very thoughtful questions about specific things that he was facing for which I might have insight to share with him. I was having so much fun talking to him—and helping him solve actionable problems that he was facing—that I let the hour go into two-plus hours and told him I'd love to set up regular calls with him. He followed up later that week with a brief update on what actions he had taken and the resulting outcomes. He eventually did ask me to set up monthly mentorship calls, but he's always respected my time—even to the point that I have to repeatedly tell him to come to me earlier and more often when he's facing something—and he always thoughtfully considers the advice I give. Plus, he's just a genuinely good guy and I enjoy my time with him. In short order, he became someone I was very much willing to spend my time mentoring, and he has now become a member of my own kitchen cabinet. And he never asked me to mentor him—it just happened naturally.

When we overlay the invisible rule book beyond the written rules, we begin to grasp how to get to baseline success. It provides some essential layering, but these two aspects alone aren't wholly sufficient. You're now at the threshold that unlocks expectations and sets the Unruly course for breakout success.

3

PAY NO ATTENTION TO THE MAN BEHIND THE CURTAIN

I n this social media–infused world, many people present themselves as something they're not. They're filtered; they're airbrushed; they're stylized. In the case of AI and deepfakes, they might not even be a person. I feel sometimes like we're living in the world of the Great and Powerful Oz. But remember "pay no attention to the man behind the curtain"? So often, there's a metaphorical person behind the curtain in people's lives, and what's happening on the surface—what we can see— doesn't match what's happening in real life behind the curtain. So, beyond the written and unwritten rules, there's a whole lot that goes on that is even harder to see or interpret, but having instinct and understanding about what you don't see is critical to breakout success.

This chapter takes on the things behind the curtain, the things that people don't want you to see—and perhaps haven't even recognized in themselves. But in understanding the basic psychological and moral principles behind this duality of what's real and what's packaged—by forcing yourself to be introspective about your own drivers and the possible hidden drivers of others—you can capitalize on putting together a larger picture than what is shown and distinguish yourself within that context.

THOUGHTFUL AUTHENTICITY

"Authenticity" is a major buzzword lately; *Merriam-Webster* made "authentic" the "word of the year" in 2023. There is, likewise, a recent movement to "bring your whole self to work." But just like the problems that come from the filtered, airbrushed, stylized version that we see from many in social media, this lay-it-all-out-there version can be problematic as well. As in pretty much everything in life, the magic is in the balance between the two extremes.

Let's call that balance "thoughtful authenticity," or authenticity that keeps the core of *you* but recognizes the social and professional contexts in which we all live and work. Thoughtful authenticity captures the credibility that can be lost when you are laying everything out there at all times with no thought to the context, and it brings the benefits of stronger relationships, better psychological health, more effective work outcomes from closer-knit teams, higher social status, and overall better health.

So how do we cultivate thoughtful authenticity? There are four pillars that are critical to generating that balance.

The first is **executive presence,** which is, at its core, just recognizing the norms and expectations for how you present yourself in different situations and modulating your self-presentation accordingly. You absolutely shouldn't be exactly the same in every single interaction you have. On any given day, I may present myself as a daughter to a mom with advanced Alzheimer's (and my presentation will be different in interacting with her and interacting with her doctor); as a mom trying to get my kids to do their homework on time or clean their room; and as a thought leader to a group of CEOs in a keynote speech. In each of these situations, I'm presenting myself authentically, but the parts of myself that I'm highlighting and the way that I'm speaking and interacting will necessarily differ. I'm not hiding any parts of myself, but I'm certainly not bringing every single part of myself to the forefront in every interaction I have. You couldn't possibly do that, so you're already picking and choosing which parts are activated. Executive presence just asks you to be thoughtful in which parts of yourself you are highlighting in which interactions.

The second pillar is **showing behind that curtain**—showing the reality behind what is presented on the surface but balancing the mess with the good parts of you: your successes and achievements. Too many people end up showing the chaos without finding ways to show the impressive parts. Maybe they feel like showing those impressive parts is bragging or somehow untoward. Certainly, the conditioning of females over the years has been to downplay our achievements lest someone believe that we are too full of ourselves. We sacrifice our own ego for the good of the relationship and making other people feel good about themselves. But if being authentic is always showing the mess and never showing the wins, it undercuts our credibility. We never see the inspiration in the person, just the hot mess. That doesn't serve any of us well.

The third and fourth pillars both come from classic psychology and research from the 1960s. Elliot Aronson, who is probably best known for his research on cognitive dissonance along with Leon Festinger, also did a series of experiments in the mid-1960s on something he called the "pratfall effect." Basically, he measured the impact of a small "pratfall"—like spilling a cup of coffee or tripping, something cringey and embarrassing but not catastrophic—on measures of likability and competence. The impression of someone who experienced a pratfall was better than if they performed perfectly—the pratfall improved how they were perceived. But this held true only if they had established their credibility in advance of the pratfall. For those with lower credibility, the pratfall lowered their likability evaluations.

So, from the pratfall effect, we learn: **establish your credibility up front** and *then* show your authenticity.

The last pillar comes from some research that Bob Cialdini recounts in his seminal book *Influence*. He argues that one of the principles of influence is authority. However, central to this idea of authenticity, one of the best ways to establish your credibility is through **credible authority**. Essentially, this just means that you own up to your mistakes and weaknesses before someone else can discover them. Admitting to a mistake when you don't have to—when it hasn't yet been discovered—makes you trustworthy. If you pair that with your authority, you've established a stronger presence than a perfect persona, because people recognize that what you're saying can be trusted, since you'll own up to the weaknesses or the mistakes when they exist.

An up-and-coming business owner that I am lucky to mentor is the perfect example of thoughtful authenticity. When you first meet TJ, he looks straight out of central casting as a Marine, even though he was actually in the Air Force, and a graduate of the prestigious military college the Citadel. He's got a long, bushy beard and huge muscles and full-sleeve tattoos. My daughter was shocked when she met him because she didn't think I could be good friends with someone as cool as TJ (because obviously, I'm not nearly that cool in her mind). Before TJ ever opens his mouth, you think you know just what he's going to be like.

Except he's entirely the opposite of what you'd expect. He's soft-spoken and infuses the conversation with mindfulness concepts and mental health considerations. He's humble and not afraid to show vulnerability. He talks openly about his struggles with post-traumatic stress. He's brilliant, having worked on complex academic issues with MITRE, one of the premier government think tanks. He makes no apologies for exactly who he is, even when some of the people he talks to would feel much more comfortable with him playing to the stereotypes. It makes TJ a remarkable leader (and a phenomenal friend). TJ doesn't hide any part of himself, and because of his ability to fit into so many different contexts authentically and easily, he opens doors for himself and his firm.

DOING THE WRONG THING PAYS OFF
(BUT STILL DO THE RIGHT THING)

One of the biggest drivers of our company's success was having a clear purpose—the "why" behind our efforts—that wasn't solely or even predominantly profit driven. I never saw profits as bad, certainly, but honestly, I never saw profit as the reason behind the firm. The firm was founded simply because there weren't professional-level jobs for military spouses on the base in Italy; this was another way of continuing to serve the government mission. As I said earlier, naming the firm was hard, but the motto—Putting Good Government into Practice—came immediately and never changed because it made up the core of our why.

We were willing to forego clear profits if their pursuit didn't meet our moral compass, or if we thought we couldn't perform up to our high standards. The funny thing was, in so doing, I am convinced that we saw much higher overall profits in the long term than we would have—than many competitor firms did—by pursuing profits more directly.

One early example of this was in a competition for professional office work in strategy and planning for a base the Navy was significantly expanding in Djibouti, Africa, a strategic priority for the military. There were two firms—us and another small business—that both had similar contracts in the same office that was going to be consolidated, so that only one firm would win a larger contract and the other firm would be forced out. We put in our proposal and heard that we were going to win the contract, but then the other firm blatantly cheated, and it looked like they might get away with it and beat us.

I called my brother, apoplectic. How could a firm that was so obviously cheating potentially win? My brother, likely chuckling inside at the naïveté of his little sister, told me that *of course* cheating works. If it didn't, people wouldn't do it. Let me say that again:

If doing the wrong thing didn't pay off, people would never do the wrong thing.

So simple, so clear, and yet I didn't intuit that until my brother said it. Of course, cheating works. If it didn't, why would people cheat or do anything else against the rules? If cutting corners in ways that impacted safety didn't pay off, nobody would ever cut corners. If doing anything that is objectively and clearly not the "right" thing didn't gain you some advantage (money, power, status, whatever), everyone would always do the right thing and there'd be no rule breaking. We have a legal system in place to hold lawbreakers accountable, which clearly shows that people do break the rules, so obviously people don't automatically do the "right" thing.

But then my brother said something else, and it was just as profound (and simple). He told me that I wasn't built to cheat, and that I needed to be able to sleep at night. My moral compass wouldn't allow me to break the actual rules, and that might mean that I left some opportunities on the table that other, less scrupulous people might take advantage of. And that was okay. Not only okay, but the only path that could possibly be right for me. It is the path where I am 100 percent comfortable with losing out on immediate gains to follow what I know to be right. I remembered this conversation countless times throughout my professional career— particularly when people were calling me a sucker for not

crossing clear boundaries or for not doing what others did
without another thought.

I think the fact that I never saw the company as a pri-
marily profit driven one was our saving grace in most of our
decisions. Our motto truly defined our mission. When there
was a gray area—and there were many over the years—I'd ask
myself if doing something would go against our "good government" purpose. **Our purpose was easy, it was clear, and it
was unequivocal.** We were in this to Put Good Government
into Practice. Would we do that if we proceeded with the decision in front of us? If so, let's find a way to "yes." If it went
against our good government principles, no matter how much
money it could make us, we weren't going to do it. If you have
that clarity of purpose—and that purpose isn't simply to make
money or amass power—it can be the centering function for
making the right decisions as you walk your Unruly path.

I recognize that I'm talking about this clear moral compass
as if everyone has the exact same gut check of what is right and
what is wrong. Clearly, there are people who just don't have
a well-developed moral compass, and there are also shades of
gray in what is "right" and "wrong" and what is somewhere in
the middle. Finding the legal, moral, and ethical path to the
things that fall "somewhere in the middle" is essentially the
subject of this book. I can't teach a moral compass, but the vast
majority of us, those who are not sociopaths, do have a sense of
right and wrong, and that's what I'm referring to in this "moral
compass" shorthand.

One thing I realized as the company grew was that it was
really easy to follow your morals when the stakes were low (or
when you likely would get caught if you cheated). As the stakes

for each decision became higher, as the money we made started becoming meaningful, it was easier and easier to justify why breaking your moral compass wasn't *actually* breaking your moral compass.

This goes to one of my favorite concepts in psychology, namely, cognitive dissonance. Basically, we can't hold two conflicting thoughts in our head, or take an action that conflicts with an active thought, or the highlighted disconnect between the two will produce severe agita (called "dissonance"). We generally become so unsettled by feeling that dissonance that we need to reconcile it some way or another. Generally, we will explain away how a thought and an action aren't in conflict with one another, or we'll work to make sure that we push aside our conflicting thoughts so that they're not active in our head when we're taking a conflicting action. That first time you break through a clear line drawn by your moral compass, you end up justifying that the line is not *here* but actually *there* instead. Or that the rule you're breaking isn't really a critical rule, or not as clear cut as you originally thought. You've reduced your cognitive dissonance and allowed yourself to cross that line.

And once you break through one line, the next ones become easier and easier to cross. I saw leaders fall prey to this trap again and again. I almost fell prey to it myself a time or two, although luckily, I had enough strong advisors around me who would call me out on things if they saw it, and I learned early to trust the twinge in my gut that would become a massive stomachache if I was crossing lines, and I always righted myself. I never came close to crossing the big lines, but there were plenty of things that were in the gray. There were things like a government person recommending someone for us to hire. Sometimes that was fine, and in fact very much welcome, if the person being recommended was fully qualified, and we were conducting a search and would consider them along with others. And sometimes it was obvious that you couldn't and shouldn't hire them, in cases where they weren't qualified or were related to the government official or the official made it a quid pro quo. But the nuances in between, where we had to weigh if it was an unreasonable request or just great networking, is where I found myself trusting both my gut and the advisors around me.

IMPOSTER SYNDROME AS YOUR SUPERPOWER

Just like authenticity, the term "imposter syndrome" is widespread. In a nutshell, imposter syndrome is when high-achieving people (mostly women) feel like they're not really deserving of their success, and that at some point, the world will discover that they're not really as impressive as everyone thinks they are, and they'll be unmasked as an imposter. There are countless books and talks and coaching businesses dedicated entirely to those who suffer from imposter syndrome, and yet it still feels like the shame of imposter syndrome hamstrings so many high-achieving people throughout their career—and their life overall. But what if we can bring it out from behind the curtain, remove the shame that comes with imposter syndrome, and instead turn it into a superpower?

I first heard the term during my first year in my PhD program at Dartmouth in 1995. We would host brown-bag lunches with professors from other universities routinely, and one of the very first brown-bag speakers was a woman who had been doing research for decades on imposter syndrome. And while the term is widespread in nonacademic literature and pop culture now, in the mid-1990s it was only starting to get noticed in the psychology literature and rarely in popular literature, even though the research had started in the 1970s.

So, in 1995, I sat in a conference room in Silsby Hall at Dartmouth, in the company of a bunch of old men and one woman in the audience, and I shrunk down into my chair, absolutely petrified that they were going to discover that—contrary to the central thesis of the theory that the achievement was, in fact, well deserved—I was *actually* the imposter. Wow, did I miss the point of the talk that day—and for some years to come.

I spent most of my early to midtwenties waiting to be discovered as a fraud. It probably didn't help that my graduate school advisor, Todd, routinely told me as much—that I didn't deserve to be there, that I wasn't smart enough to cut it in academia, that I was never going to finish my PhD, that everyone else in the lab was smarter and more successful than me. I remember my first week in graduate school, when Todd told me that he was like a Marine Corps drill sergeant, and he was going to break me down from the person I was and build me back up into his image. I called my best friend that night, crying at what I had gotten myself into and saying "but I don't want to be a fat, sweaty, old man!" It should probably be noted that Todd was maybe thirty-two or thirty-three at the time, so decidedly not "old," although to my credit he was hopelessly out of shape and would get winded and sweaty going up a flight of stairs.

Years later, Todd and two other professors were the subject of a $70 million lawsuit for sexual harassment and abuse, and Dartmouth ended up settling for $14 million and banning them all from campus for life, which was finally my proof that karma does, indeed, come back around. But at the time, he was all-powerful as my graduate advisor and seemed all-knowing, so his insults cut deeply and made me question everything about myself.

I carried that feeling of being an imposter on to my first year in the White House, when I had half a dozen accounts across the federal government, from Education to Labor to Housing, and everyone seemed to know their issues dramatically better than I ever could. There I was, with an Ivy League PhD and a White House badge, thinking that everyone around me had made a mistake in "letting" me in, because I was clearly a total poseur.

I've read a lot over the years about the perils of imposter syndrome, and there's an entire cottage industry around getting over it. Certainly, some advice about owning your seat at the table, changing negative self-talk, and managing perfectionism can be really helpful, particularly in your early career or during a time of change or pressure in your life.

Recently, however, I've realized that maybe imposter syndrome itself isn't really a problem and may indeed be a major driver of success. Stay with me here, because this turns the last thirty-plus years of conventional wisdom on its head. There's a secret, and once you discover it, it really does promote imposter syndrome into a superpower instead of a liability. Ready?

Good leaders don't know what they're doing a good portion of the time.

That's not to say that they can't figure it out, or they don't have the tools to get their job done, but if a leader knows (or seems to know) what they're doing all or even most of the time, they generally fall into one of three traps, and none of these will a good leader make:

1. They're not pushing hard enough and therefore staying within a comfort zone that won't allow for real growth.
2. They're overconfident and don't know what they don't know.
3. They're faking it, and at least subconsciously they know they don't know but they're too terrified to admit it (even to themselves).

In other words, the truth about imposter syndrome is that everyone will sometimes feel like an imposter if they're trying to perform at high levels. Women are more likely to "suffer" from imposter syndrome mostly because they tend to be better at self-reflection and recognize it, whereas many men don't understand that they don't know what they're doing or why they're feeling uncomfortable. The earlier you figure out that everyone is at least sometimes making this up as they go along, the earlier you realize that you've got this. The problem isn't that you're an imposter, the problem is that you don't recognize that everyone else is generally making this up too. If you are succeeding at high levels, there are almost never any easy answers. There is no clear-cut path forward or else everyone would be on the same path. So that feeling of being an imposter is just a feeling of uncertainty, which is exactly how you should feel when you're pushing boundaries.

Being comfortable with imposter syndrome isn't to say that you shouldn't work to own your seat at the table, that you shouldn't question your internal negative self-talk, that you shouldn't stand in front of the mirror and give yourself positive affirmations (although I've never been able to do that with a straight face). It just means that, once you realize everyone you likely respect has been in the same boat, imposter syndrome becomes a tool you can use to seek advice and counsel easily and make the best decisions possible, rather than a weakness you have to overcome. You need to **get comfortable in your own discomfort**. It is only in this discomfort that growth happens. Complacency is comfortable, but it doesn't foster a growth mindset. Much of the advice around combatting imposter syndrome focuses on getting you out of your own discomfort. Instead, learning to live with the discomfort, own the discomfort, and realize that the discomfort is where growth happens is the secret to truly combatting imposter syndrome.

But that also doesn't mean you *just* live with the discomfort. Recognizing that feeling of discomfort should lead you to introspection and motivate you to seek information and guidance. Owning this discomfort means admitting it and finding ways to overcome it proactively and productively. Those living in this gray area have to be fully authentic and able to seek help to learn what they don't know. You have to admit your limitations. You have to be open to real feedback. And you need a knowledgeable, expert support system around you—your concentric circles and your kitchen cabinet—that can provide honest feedback in a way that is insightful, useful, and actionable.

As noted above, there are three traps that people fall into when they don't experience imposter syndrome, at least not as traditionally conceived. None of the people falling into these traps make good leaders, and all of them are less likely to be successful than those who do experience imposter syndrome but don't suffer from it. Embracing the imposter within you can then supercharge your success, rather than be a liability. Let's look at each of these types of traps.

The first trap *is not pushing outside of their comfort zone.* When I first got out of graduate school, my brother told me something that has stuck with me for the last twenty-five years. I was looking at job opportunities, and I kept telling him that I wasn't qualified because I hadn't done *X, Y,* or *Z* in the job posting. He said, quite simply, "If you've done everything you're going to do in the new job before, you're looking at the wrong job." In other words, every job should be a combination of skill sets you've already developed along with new challenges. If you can easily do the job, you're not pushing hard enough.

I took it to heart when, in interviewing for my job at the White House, my eventual boss asked me why he should hire me with a PhD in psychology when everyone else had a background in economics and I had never taken a single class in it. My response was that psychology and economics are both social science disciplines with the same basic rules and tools. I was an expert in those tools, and the details were the details—I could learn them. It must have worked, because I got the job. (That was definitely a fake-it-until-you-make-it moment, because I didn't have that confidence at the time, but I channeled my big brother and acted like I did, and it worked.)

I took it to heart, as well, when building the company. That first opportunity was in Anti-Terrorism/Force Protection. My background was in domestic social policy, and I knew almost nothing about the military from a professional perspective. And this wasn't even the business or policy side of the military, which at least somewhat aligned with what I knew well from my OMB days. This was "guns, guards, and gates"—how to operationally protect our most critical assets for our military in a time of war. But it was built upon all the skills I had learned at OMB about leveraging my own strengths and relying on experts for their knowledge. I knew how to track budgets and align strategy and policy with on-ground execution, and how to measure outcomes to ensure operational success. I had people around me who were the subject matter experts that I'd be working with, and I knew I was smart enough and motivated enough to learn the details quickly and effectively to incorporate their knowledge with my skills. I took the leap and continued to take those leaps throughout the life of the firm. Throughout the firm's history, we never pushed so far outside of our comfort zone that we couldn't easily learn the details or hire people who could execute with our leadership and management, but at each turn, we took another step or two outside of our comfort zone and gained knowledge and experience that paid off. And that not only took me out of feeling like an imposter in the moment, but it got me comfortable with that feeling going forward, because I knew it was just a temporary signal that I needed to learn more.

The only way to grow is to keep pushing yourself. It is easy to become complacent and continue to do what you know how to do. Learning only takes place when you aren't doing the same thing you already do repeatedly. Certainly, you can't

push yourself on every single aspect of your life all the time—
that's a recipe for burnout. But if you look around and wonder
why some people with the same raw talent and opportunities
achieve breakout success when others just end up doing fine,
more than likely you'll see the über successful person taking
risks—failing more, but also succeeding more. Sheer force of
will and grit—working harder than anyone else—will get you
far, but not if you're just working harder while doing the same
thing repeatedly.

The second trap is *not knowing what they don't know*.
I can't count the number of overconfident people I've seen in
business, or in my White House days, or in academia. It used
to intimidate me to run across these supremely confident people—because I believed their hype. They always seemed to
know *so* much more than me, and every interaction with them
would just fuel my imposter syndrome that much more.

This is the stereotypical "mansplainer" who speaks with
confidence about every issue, even those that they have no
business speaking with confidence about. They're not faking
it, at least not consciously. They truly have the ego to believe
that they really are smarter than everyone else in the room, on
every issue out there. They won't seek out guidance from people smarter than them, because they can't conceive that anyone
could possibly be smarter than them.

The last trap *is faking it, even to themselves*. Too often,
leaders present this image of the all-knowing, unflappable, perfect person. There is nobody—nobody—whose life is as perfect
as they present. Social media has just made this worse than it
was when I was coming up the ranks in my early career, but it
has always been true. Very few people will show you the mess

behind the curtain of their lives. But some people cling hard to the image they present, even to the point that they use psychological strategies to fool themselves into thinking they're confident and correct.

I had one colleague who, every time he made a mistake, would claim that he meant to make the mistake and give a reason behind it. No, he didn't mean to make the mistake—that was obvious to everyone around him. The mistake itself didn't matter, but not owning up to it lost him credibility every time he did it, and therefore he lost the trust of those working for him. He was particularly bad at faking it, but the lesson holds even for those whose bravado is more nuanced.

It is important to note that "faking it until you make it" is absolutely a viable strategy, and one that I've used to great success in pretty much every aspect of my life at times. Paired with an acknowledgment, even internally, that you are projecting a confidence you don't feel, and particularly seeking out the information that can eventually back up your fake confidence, can be a strong technique of a leader. If you are authentically nervous all the time, nobody will think you can lead effectively.

But fake confidence can be toxic, particularly when it comes with malevolent behavior that stems from an often-unacknowledged fear of being discovered. These folks can be dangerous as leaders, because they aren't willing to admit when they don't know something, and they'll try to bluster their way through everything. This version of "faking it" yields really bad decisions, and often a negative culture all the way down the chain of command as everyone ends up tiptoeing around the leader's toxic, fragile ego and holding back relevant feedback.

CHECK YOUR EGO

Over the years, I've developed a really thick skin. I joke that I have a big enough ego that I don't need anyone else to feed it and enough imposter syndrome to continuously look for outside help to get better. In truth, my ego isn't "big" but stable. I know what I'm good at, I know what I'm not good at, and I'm eager to make myself better through feedback.

I have always been one to seek feedback, possibly to the extreme. In college, every single psychology class I took had some discussion about "groupthink," and it always centered around the NASA *Challenger* disaster, where the brilliant NASA engineers, striving for consensus over critical thinking and alternate viewpoints, overlooked clear danger signals leading up to launch day, leading to the midair explosion and death of all astronauts on board. Avoiding groupthink was so burned into my psyche that I suppose I went to the other extreme to seek out differing views and not construct defense mechanisms to critical feedback. Not only do I welcome that feedback, but I also recognize it as the mark of a committed, engaged employee. I tell all my employees—repeatedly—that I won't always take their feedback, but it is their job to make sure I've heard it. I've had employees tell me after trying and failing to get my attention about something they thought was critical: "Boss, I'm going to try one more time to make sure you hear what I have to say, because I think you're about to make a mistake, but if you tell me today that you've heard me, I'll move out on whatever you say." Most times, they were right that I didn't hear them, and when I did, we changed course.

This takes a strong and stable ego, and comfort with your own abilities so that you don't feel threatened by the feedback. With a strong and stable ego, feedback can feel constructive. With any instability in your ego, that feedback can feel like an attack. If you find yourself getting defensive about feedback, take a step back and ask yourself if there's a way you could look at it as helpful guidance instead of criticism, even if you don't think it was meant that way. If you can assume that it was meant productively, and the giver has your best interests at heart, you might hear it very differently. Even in the case where you know they meant it as criticism, if you can strip away the barbs and ask yourself if there are any nuggets in there that could be useful, you might come away from a bad interaction with some good takeaways. Or not, if the person is simply a bad actor. Then feel free to dismiss every bit of negative feedback!

I didn't realize quite the extreme I took this to until we had a new senior employee join the team during a critical change management project we were undertaking. We put out some interim guidance to the senior team and got back a long email from one of our long-standing vice presidents with over a dozen detailed questions about the guidance that he hoped we could answer as we finalized our path forward. I thought nothing of it, said I would keep that list handy as we finalized the guidance (because it was a darn good list of relevant questions), and I moved on with my day. The new senior employee called me, mortified that someone who worked for me would talk to me that disrespectfully—where I saw it as a sign of huge respect that my VP had taken the time to really dig in and help me work through my guidance to make it better.

It struck me that I clearly do things differently than most people out there. Although it isn't necessary that everyone be quite *that* open to critical feedback, and it certainly takes significant trust on both sides to make that type of feedback loop work, it might be one of the most important secrets to my personal path to success. I believe strongly that encouraging my team's tough questions made us better as leaders and made the firm perform better every time.

Good leaders never want to be the smartest person in the room—but they also know they're smart enough to keep up with everyone there and learn from them. Their egos are strong enough to let them take advice from anyone and everyone. Their superpower of imposter syndrome allows them to understand they can't know everything and want to continuously get smarter. They also recognize that asking for advice—and listening intently to that advice, although not blindly taking any advice without filtering it through their own leadership expertise—is another easy way to build trust with their employees. Better decisions with more trust from your staff? Yes, please.

When we look at ego, we can look it across three axes:

1. Level of self-esteem (high or low)
2. Stability of self-esteem (stable or variable)
3. Validity of self-assessments (valid or invalid)

Obviously, someone can have high views of themselves on some aspects and low on others, but for ease of discussion, we'll look at this globally. At the most basic, someone with reasonably high, stable self-esteem is clearly the most well adjusted and successful as compared to someone with any other combination. They can generally know what they're good at and not good at, and act accordingly.

Someone with consistently low self-esteem can be difficult to spend time with and obviously can have some challenges in achievement. But it is those with the most variable self-esteem who are generally the most challenging to interact with, *particularly* those with the highest self-esteem. In short, this is because of the way they react to ego threats—those things that challenge their view of themselves. These are the people who don't suffer from imposter syndrome because they're faking it even to themselves. Instead, everyone around them suffers from their fragile ego.

Someone with high, stable self-esteem, or even middle-of-the-road but stable self-esteem, is mostly nonplussed when they're told that they did something wrong. They can generally take feedback and incorporate it—or dismiss it if they think it isn't apropos—and move on. Someone with high-variable self-esteem lashes out when faced with something that threatens their positive self-views. These are the worst of the toxic leaders; they can't take constructive feedback from anyone without looking to undercut those around them. These are the folks that assume all their success is well deserved and everyone else just got lucky. And they can make it to a leadership role often because they're good at managing up, by kissing up even as they punch down on their direct reports.

The third axis is how valid the view of yourself is. Someone who has an inflated self-esteem compared to their actual accomplishments is particularly toxic, and we see more and more of this in the "everybody gets a trophy" world we've lived in over the last few decades. These leaders are also most likely to react poorly to ego threats, because they don't have the solid underpinnings for their ego. Their ego is fragile because it isn't based on actual, tangible accomplishments.

I would also add a fourth consideration to this analysis, something called "rumination" in psychology literature, or how quickly you can move on or keep thinking about negative feedback (or anything else negative, for that matter). My kids' hockey coach had a much more colorful way of describing it than I'd seen in academic papers: Be like Dory (the fish from *Finding Nemo*). He told me that the best players had to be Dory-like and forget a bad play as soon as it was over, so that they could be ready to handle the next play. The more you ruminate on something that goes wrong—particularly on an ego threat—the more damaging the ego threat will be. If you take it in, incorporate it or dismiss it, and move on, no problem. If you turn it over and over in your mind, particularly if you have unstable self-esteem, it yields increasingly more toxic results.

So, to the extent that you can be honest about your strengths and weaknesses and guard against the massive pendulum swings from ego threats, and move on quickly from those ego threats, the better you will be (in hockey and in leadership).

UNMASK THE MAN BEHIND THE CURTAIN

All of these "behind the curtain" issues share one common thread. They can be managed most effectively with introspection; with knowing yourself, your thoughts and feelings, your motivations, your unconscious biases and knee-jerk reactions.

Effectively harnessing thoughtful authenticity, imposter syndrome as a superpower, and following your moral compass all take a firm grounding in knowing yourself well, actively examining your thoughts and feelings in every situation, and finding ways to react appropriately.

Some of that is well beyond the scope of this book, but is still critically important work to do, either by yourself or with a therapist or executive coach. But chapter 6 does give some clear and actionable ways to get introspective in some of the most common situations you find yourself in as you start challenging the rules.

Part 2

CHALLENGE THE RULES

The young man knows the rules, but the old man knows the exceptions.

—Oliver Wendell Holmes Sr.

4

THE UNRULY PLAYBOOK

In building WWC Global, we were blazing what felt like an entirely new path, and we quickly realized that doing the same thing in the same way as everyone else wasn't going to get us anywhere. We knew we had to comply with the laws and regulations around government contracts without question—but we were told there were unwritten rules, which was "the way everyone did things." We created our own paths by finding a better way when we couldn't come up with a good answer as to why everyone did something a certain way.

We heard over and over: "But that's not how it is done." Okay, fair. That's *not* how it *has been* done in the past. In each case, we'd ask ourselves if something *should* be done the same way that everyone else did it. Just a small sampling of the things we heard weren't the way things were done:

- Military spouses couldn't possibly do high-level consulting, policy, or program-management work. They don't have the background, and you can't train them. Plus, they move around too much, and most of them don't have the education or work history to do the work. This one always felt like a throwback to my mom's generation to me; we were fighting the same lingering and outdated stereotypes that the rest of the professional world had thrown out thirty-plus years before.

- You need a centralized office in one geographic location, and all back-office employees need to report there every day. It's impossible to keep people on board while they move around and too difficult to keep track of what they're doing while working from home. After Covid, this argument has changed, but in 2005, remote work was revolutionary.

- Women who haven't been in the military, and specifically in operational roles, can't possibly oversee an operationally focused contract, particularly at the elite level of Special Operations Command staffed with former operators like SEALs and Special Forces. They won't understand the subject matter because they haven't lived it, and the operators won't respect them.

- Profit must be the central driver of business. You can't possibly succeed in business if you don't focus on profit as the primary metric.

We were forced to look at every rule, every entry point, every crossroads differently because we were, well, different. Our differentiator came through acknowledging that, leveraging it, and pushing back on what everyone else accepted as truth. By showing them that we were better for doing it differently than everyone else, we succeeded not *in spite of* conventional wisdom, but *because* we upended it. But we had to deliver to make that potential a reality.

So, we got Unruly.

Getting Unruly meant finding the places where the rules have room for interpretation, space for innovation, seams to leverage. Those places allowed us to distinguish ourselves to find our own success. The true magic in an Unruly path comes in understanding the rules so well that you know where you can push to challenge whatever has been held as the conventional wisdom.

Throughout twenty years of war in Afghanistan, we had hundreds of thousands of Afghanis helping our US forces, often at great personal risk to themselves and their families. There is a process, using what are called SIVs (Special Immigrant Visas), to allow these heroes to immigrate to the US or another ally country, but the process is cumbersome and time-consuming, and many SIV-eligible people were still waiting, at various stages in the process, when we pulled out of Afghanistan. Throughout the war, in every single presidential administration from Bush 2 to Biden, I watched countless military members become Unruly to sponsor the Afghanis who had served alongside them and saved their lives. They learned the rules, they knew how the real "game" worked, and they were tireless in their advocacy, and the vast majority of SIV holders came through because of the steadfast dedication of military members and their ceaseless efforts. During the pullout from Afghanistan in 2021, well over one hundred thousand SIV-eligible Afghanis were still in-country and at grave risk. Enter an Unruly group of veterans who work in what they call the "gray space" of contingency operations, where the government can't or won't act to evacuate. These veterans, most of them former special operators like my friend Andy (a former Delta Force operator) and Sean (the former Commander of the Navy SEALs), worked tirelessly to navigate the complex rules of international law, the practical considerations of logistics, and the gray space of non-state diplomacy to rescue thousands of our allies. Since the Afghanistan airlift, they've continued their efforts in the Ukraine, Sudan, Haiti, and other natural and manmade disasters. They are truly a group of Unruly heroes.

This part of the book is designed to give you tools to know when, where, and how to push within the rules effectively. These are certainly not the only tools you may discover as you push on those boundaries that make sense for you. Being Unruly is much more nuanced than breaking rules. It requires you to *always refer back to the rules* when you're looking at opportunities to change up the way the game is played. These Unruly tools are applicable in any situation, through all the roles you play. Use these tools when you're working through parenting issues, when you're going through challenges with your spouse, when you're trying to find equilibrium among all aspects of your life. These Unruly tools can change your perspective and help you find a way in and through all aspects of your life.

One of the first times I saw the Unruly process play out was when I was in the White House, and the Bush administration had started their faith-based initiative. My boss at OMB put me on the team to help review the rules that would be necessary to implement the initiative across the government. I was the only career staffer, the only non-lawyer, and the only person on the team who hadn't clerked for a Supreme Court justice. Talk about some serious imposter syndrome at that first meeting! I also had significant reservations about the project, particularly as a Jew who had been subject to plenty of "voluntary" religion in my public school growing up. The concept was pretty straightforward, although controversial. The Constitution clearly prohibits the government funding of religious programs, but many of the social service programs are provided by faith-based organizations, and in some spaces, the faith-based providers were the only game in town. Was it possible to fund the nonreligious aspects of, say, a food pantry or an addiction-recovery program with government dollars?

We used all the tools in this chapter to explore the questions. We had some spirited discussions—and I got over my imposter syndrome quickly and spoke up loudly throughout— and (I think) we drafted some clear and reasonable guidelines. It turned out that it was pretty easy to fund a food pantry and carve out any religious aspects; less so for some addiction-recovery programs where the religious aspects were generally interwoven into the program itself. But it was possible to craft clear rules that allowed the desired novel outcome in many cases, without running afoul of the existing laws.

ASK THE TWO-YEAR-OLD'S QUESTIONS

At its heart, becoming Unruly requires us to ask the same questions that a two-year-old would ask. *Why? Why not? Why can't I? Who says so?* If we rely on this process, while always going back to the source documents to see if there are any answers that *do* block us from doing what we want, we start to distinguish ourselves while navigating to the blue water instead of heading into red water or drifting into black water.

I learned the value of questioning conventional wisdom in my White House days. People would tell me definitively that "you can't do" something, whatever that specific "something" was. They'd tell me it was either not the way things were done, or that it was against the rules, or that it wouldn't work for some other reason. Once I got over my imposter syndrome and realized that most everyone was blustering their way through much more than they let on, I got comfortable asking these basic questions. Sometimes they had good answers. Oftentimes, they had reasonable answers that couldn't withstand the slightest challenge, because they were just based on the way things always were done and nobody had thought to ever question it. Sometimes, they had no answer other than "I said so," which doesn't work for two-year-olds, and it certainly doesn't work in a professional setting.

Using the two-year-old's mentality is key to unlocking Unruly opportunities. It is essentially just a tool to bring us back to the basics and ask if things need to keep happening the way they always have. It asks what might happen if we try something new.

To be sure, asking the question isn't about proving yourself to be right and it doesn't presuppose the answer. Some of the questions that two-year-olds ask—and some of the questions you may ask—are absolute nonstarters. It doesn't mean you shouldn't ask the question, but it does mean that you should be ready for the answer to be a valid reason that you can't do something. That's okay. In fact, that's good, because it reinforces that the rule, whether written or unwritten, has reasonable logic applied. Gathering information about what's possible can lead you to other options, other tools, other crazy ideas that might just work.

But like any two-year-old asks repeatedly (over and over and OVER), so should you. Don't take the first no as definitive. Get to the actual ground truth, where a no is actually conclusive. And then get to the deeper understanding of *why* the no is really a no, and if there are any ways to get creative. We'll get into those creative ways around the actual no later in this chapter, but you can and should start with getting just slightly annoyed in asking and pushing hard using the two-year-old's questions.

If you are experiencing imposter syndrome, this might be a very uncomfortable exercise. Asking these basic questions can make you feel like you're exposing your own ignorance. Once you use the tools from the last chapter to convert imposter syndrome into your superpower, it becomes less uncomfortable, but another trick to make it easier is to couch it as a thought experiment. *Let's strip this down to the fundamentals and think differently; at the most basic, is there a different way to approach this?* This way, you're not actively challenging anyone's authority or beliefs, and you're not exposing that you don't know something. It makes it a much more collaborative and often thought-provoking exercise.

I've found that, particularly in government, many people automatically say no just to see how persistent you are. The vast majority of people will stop at the first no, throw up their hands, and give up. It is a pretty ingenious way of cutting down on workload—just deny everyone, and only look closely if they complain. This isn't just a technique in the government,

to be sure. Plenty of other industries—or even personal relationships—do the same. Again, act like a two-year-old in this
instance. If you've ever spent much time with a two-year-old,
or even a teenager, you'll know that the repeated attempts to
change your mind may frustrate you, but often they work. You
can be polite and respectful in your pursuit, and often your
persistence and approaching multiple sources with the same
query can pay off.

GO TO THE SOURCE

As you're asking those questions, there's a second set of questions that should follow—also reminiscent of a two-year-old.
Show me.

Ask for the source documentation: *Show me* the black-letter
law. *Show me* the policy. *Show me* the standard that says I can't
do that.

Once you get to the ground truth of what the actual rules
say, you can start looking at if there is room for challenge, for
other interpretations. You can determine that the rules don't
actually preclude it. Or you can, indeed, determine that this
option is a nonstarter and pursue a different option. All these
pathways are valuable, and what you find can direct you in
ways that will save time, money, and other resources.

Often these "rules" are just the way things have been done
and don't have any basis in law or even guidance or best practice. They're just how someone taught my mentor, who taught
me, and now I'm teaching you, so they've taken on the veneer
of a rule without actually being a rule. Very few people truly

understand the rules themselves, and certainly not how to read and interpret or even find the rules. They just go off the gut checks they learned as they were coming up in their industry. Their understanding is apocryphal.

Once you've learned how to go to the source documents, and to understand those real rules and the interpretations of the rules, you can ask the questions of those rules, those laws, those policies, and determine what they truly say, rather than relying on the conventional wisdom of people's interpretations or guidance.

This is why it is often so resource intensive to challenge the status quo, because it takes a whole lot of research to make sure that you've found all the relevant source documents, the right case law, the right policy documents for the specific situation you're talking about. Just doing a cursory review of a few relevant standards, without the full deep dive that we discussed in chapter 1, can give you a false sense of security—or a false sense of doom. But wow, when you get good at finding the relevant standards and interpreting them, you can turn the conventional wisdom on its head. Being Unruly takes work—but doing it right can really supercharge your success.

Because it *is* so resource intensive, you shouldn't take an Unruly approach to every single thing in business or in life. It only makes sense when the return on investment of your time and other resources pays off in the dividend you'll get. Most things can follow the standard playbook without an issue. The Unruly approach should be used *only* for those critical differentiators that will lead you effectively into blue water.

You might also find that something *is* written policy somewhere, but it is able to be waived through some series of fairly easily achievable steps. Some position that is being hired for may say that it requires a master's degree, for example, but the hiring official can waive it if they certify that the candidate's extra work experience beyond the minimum required in the position description is the equivalent of a master's. Or the employee handbook says you can only fly on the cheapest flight available, but you can account for the cost of the traveler's time in determining if a flight with multiple stops is more cost effective than a direct flight in the long run. This can happen even with black-letter law instead of lower-level policies. The black-letter law may say that you're not allowed to participate in a particular government program unless you meet a very specific standard. But lo and behold, when you go to the agency's website, you find there's a demonstration project or a waiver program that specifically allows you to participate in the program.

There's no one trick to finding these exemptions—it takes some good research skills, and perseverance, and often some luck. It takes asking, and asking again, and then asking again, to the people who know the program best, if there's any wiggle room or any way you can get to your desired outcome in a different way than they've seen before. The same tools that you used for your initial research into the rules—copious use of creative search terms, following references through to the next reference and the next one after that, not taking the first no for an answer—will also come in handy as you search for these exemptions to the rules.

What everyone knows to be true may only be partially true—or true but nuanced in practice. You will be amazed at how often just doing your own research using the document that initially set the standard, which has now been interpreted and reinterpreted, will yield you a very clear and definitive answer that contradicts what everyone else has adopted and believes is black-letter law.

Let me relate an example of how we approached this in applying for a government program called 8(a) that ended up being a critical turning point in our corporate trajectory. We had heard for years that women didn't qualify for this specific "small disadvantaged business" program unless they were also part of another underrepresented group (race, ethnicity, national origin status). We accepted that truism for years. But then we looked closely at the rules themselves, and at all the case law and written guidance we could find about the program. It turned out that women weren't *often* accepted into the program based on gender alone, but that they could be if the majority owner met certain markers for discrimination. There were very clear guidelines for a binary determination of acceptance into the program. After experiencing significant gender-based challenges at Dartmouth and within the military contracting space by that point, we knew that I met those markers, and then some, so we got to work.

We wrote a compelling, well-researched and well-documented application for the program. Because we knew that using gender discrimination to qualify for the program fell outside of the expected norms, we made our case and thoroughly documented how we met or exceeded the written standards. We told a story that started from a broad perspective—with consistent themes that cut across different time periods and gave the readers a framework to understand the examples—but critically, we also got very detailed about specific examples to prove our case. We included black-letter law, case law, and policy guidance to justify how we met those written standards. From an Unruly perspective, it was an absolute work of art. We knew the rules better than anyone else and used them to our advantage to press our point. There was no way they could deny us based on the standards they themselves set forth.

We submitted it, and . . . they denied us. Not only did they deny us, but they sent a scathing letter that was shockingly unprofessional for a government office. So, we reviewed the program rules again and appealed the denial. And they denied us again, with even more strident language, and some assertions that were provably false. At this point, I was in my "oh really, watch me" mindset, and we were going to see this all the way through to the end, even if we didn't think we had a snowball's chance of getting approved.

Sometimes, getting Unruly can be uncomfortable for those of us who have been trained to be agreeable people pleasers. Upending and questioning the status quo isn't for the faint of heart. The status quo is set up to quash dissent, so being respectful but persistent is helpful. Keeping your cool and pressing forward is key. Challenging decisions and expectations can get you labeled a "Karen" (regardless of whether you're male or female, although women do seem to pay a higher price for the same behaviors), always asking to speak to the manager and challenging unnecessarily (and obnoxiously). I strongly believe that there is a way to approach being Unruly while still showing respect to the people around you, which is the exact opposite way of the stereotypical "Karen." It is absolutely your right to challenge the status quo. It is just not in your best interest to be a disrespectful jerk while doing it.

We eventually were set to appear before the Administrative Law Judge (ALJ), an agency review by an independent arbiter that was the final say—either they allowed us into the program or we were not getting in, and we had no additional recourse beyond this level. In this case, the Department of Justice (DOJ) lawyers, rather than the Small Business Administration (SBA) staff, were arguing the case before the ALJ. Just before the hearing was set, I got a call from the DOJ lawyer, which was definitely not standard procedure. He said that he had read through the entire case file and couldn't defend the decision by the SBA staff, so we were admitted to the program. It was a quintessential Unruly win.

THROW OUT THE STANDARD PLAYBOOK

In chapter 2, we talked about the standard playbook, the un-written but well-understood rules for how business gets done. This is how the well-educated players learned the rules of the game they've chosen to play. They take courses in different subjects and learn the black-letter law, the tools to comply with those rules, and—critically—the unwritten rules of the game. They look at case studies to see how things in their industry have gone well and where they've gone off the rails. They also learn—often just by working around people who have been doing it for years—how to dress, how to speak, and how to fit in with the industry they're approaching. These principles are absolutely useful. I'm never going to be one that says that education isn't a driver of success.

But the standard playbook often keeps you in a very tight

lane, even when you're being entrepreneurial. There's a lot of "this is the way things are done to be successful" within the standard playbook. There's a balance between blazing a new path with new tools and making life way too difficult for yourself. So, for everything in the standard playbook—the "this is the way our industry must do things" notions—we would ask the same two-year-old's questions we talked about above. *Why do we do this? Do we have to? Why do we have to?* Again, the answer was often that we absolutely didn't have to do things the way that everyone said they were done.

BUT.

The second set of questions as a follow-up was just as critical. *What do we gain by doing things differently than everyone else?* Does it provide a clear and compelling distinguisher from the other firms? If it doesn't provide a clear and compelling benefit, don't expend the energy reinventing the way things are done. Most things can benefit from following the standard playbook. Standards make things clear and easy and cause a whole lot fewer hassles. As in everything, there's a balance. You can't always follow the exact standard playbook that everyone else follows, but you also shouldn't throw out the entire thing every time just to be different. It is in consciously studying that standard playbook and weighing the costs and benefits of doing things differently in each case that you can find your own blue water.

The last piece of throwing out the standard playbook is following through and making the change to the standards and executing on the new path. Figure out how to change the standard to follow the rules and still distinguish yourself. Document it and put the right processes in place to make the change happen. *And then execute the change.* The *idea* of how to upend the process, and even the validation work you do to prove that you can upend the process, is not enough. You have to follow through, upend the process, get it implemented in the new way, and then reassess if it worked well or if it was really better to stay with the standard. Anything may be a good idea—or not—but the idea by itself won't get you there. Just like we talked about in networking, you have to start *doing* at some point early on, recognizing you won't be perfect, and you'll likely have to pivot as you go, but you can't get stuck just contemplating and learning. You have to *DO*.

When we started WWC, nobody had ever really used military spouses as a targeted hiring pool. I repeatedly heard two things—that we couldn't do it or that someone had thought of it before we had. But it turned out that, yes, we could do it— with some hard work in making sure we were in compliance with US and international laws, that is—and even if someone else had thought of it, they never followed through on it. Thinking of it doesn't get you partial credit. You actually have to execute.

THE HYBRID SOLUTION

One technique we used when looking at throwing out the standard playbook was what we called the "hybrid solution." I am a big fan of the hybrid solution. So often, people see only option A and option B. There's no in-between—it is either option A or option B. Choose one or choose the other. No other options exist.

But there are very rarely just those two options. You may be able to borrow a little bit from A and a little bit from B and add some from C and D, and make up your own X, Y, and Z.

My hybrid solutions used to drive some of the people in my firm crazy because inevitably it would cause more work than the standard option A or option B. The standard options were known and planned for and expected. They were, in essence, part of the standard playbook. And as we said, there's a great place for the standard options when they make sense, or when the hybrid solution won't differentiate what you're doing from the people taking the standard path or isn't worth the resource investment to pursue a new path. But there are times when those standard options just don't cut it.

I can't tell you how many times in any given week I was presented with two or three options, and I didn't love any of them, and I'd ask, "Is there a hybrid solution here?" So, the team and I would go to the drawing board and brainstorm the pieces we liked from each option and figure out if there was a way to take the best of each and combine it into a new path forward. And then, the key was to make sure that the hybrid solution bought you more in benefits than it cost in figuring out how to implement it.

The hybrid solution could be wonderful. I am the queen of the hybrid solution. But sometimes it's more trouble than it is worth. You need to understand the real return on investment for the hybrid solution to see if it buys you what you think it will. What will be the differential cost of implementation? Will you need customized software or other collateral? Will it be difficult to have any eventual customer buy off on it? Are there any other unintended consequences? How likely are you to realize the benefits versus a standard path forward?

That said, I saw again and again how often breakout success comes from a hybrid solution.

OUTCOMES OVER PROCESS

During the Bush (W, not HW ... or Bush 2, as we always called it) administration, there was a huge push to effectively evaluate government programs. Not that there wasn't in prior administrations, obviously, but the Bush team made a concerted effort to come up with a rating tool that would be used to drive budgeting decisions, because everything in government is driven in the end by how we fund the program. One of the most critical things that we tried to do was focus on actual outcome measures rather than output or process measures.

In short, outcomes are actual measures of what we're truly trying to accomplish with the program—self-sufficiency for jobs programs, healthy nutrition status for food programs, better health for insurance programs. The government, with its focus on compliance, is often much more concerned with process than with actual outcomes or even outputs. In other words, we might focus on whether we followed the process to enroll or disenroll someone on food stamps rather than determine the percentage of qualified people who got enrolled in food stamps (an output measure), or, better yet, how we impacted the nutrition status of food stamp–eligible people with the program (an outcome measure). For years, we focused on process measures or output measures in most government programs. Outcomes are much harder to measure and often multidimensional. But the outcomes are really what we care about, not the outputs or the process—not just in the government but across multiple industries and in life overall.

When we get Unruly, we want to determine what outcomes we eventually want and then overlay compliant, cost-effective, and human-capital-effective processes to ensure we get to those outcomes. Too often, the standard playbook will drive processes as the priority, and those processes are never examined to ensure they're leading to our outcome goals. Process matters, but outcomes matter more. In those cases, the processes drown out the real reason we are doing something, the outcome we're looking to attain. This isn't just an issue in compliance-heavy industries like GovCon; in any organization past the early entrepreneurial stages, bureaucracy is absolutely necessary for proper functioning, but it can get in the way when it isn't examined regularly.

In my career, I never saw anyone better at getting to outcomes over process than Army Special Forces (also known as Green Berets or SF) and other special operators. One of our strategic hires at WWC in 2011 was a retired SF Colonel, Joe, who always tells the best war stories. In 2002, he was the Deputy Commander of 3rd Special Forces Group, and they were deploying for six-month stints with four-month home time to turn around and deploy again for another six months. During one of their short home stints, they were resupplying the soldiers about to deploy, and they were told to take the old helmets of the group just coming back, because the contracting process would take too long to get them the upgraded helmets that had already been selected and were planned for purchase. Joe and his logistics officer were able to work directly with the manufacturer and figure out a legal way to purchase the newer helmets in time for the deployment. It definitely didn't follow standard processes, but it got the job done. On another deployment around the same time, there weren't enough pistols to provide to support personnel—a critical tool in the type of fighting they were facing. Joe and his logistics officer found out about some pistols that were being held in a warehouse because of a bureaucratic process, since they had been replaced by newer versions but were still perfectly serviceable. Joe was able to get them sent to 3rd SF Group in advance of the deployment. In both cases, being Unruly likely saved lives.

UNINTENDED CONSEQUENCES

There's a truism that "what gets measured gets managed." Metrics drive behaviors because people want to succeed, and metrics show us a clear way to get to success. But if we put into place the wrong set of outcome measures, we can drive unintended consequences. As leaders, we must be thoughtful about how our metrics might drive behavior.

When I was interviewing for my White House job, the interviewer asked me a question about measuring the effect of a government program called Welfare to Work. He asked how to measure the effectiveness of the program, and he was looking for a very simple answer of how many people moved from cash benefits to a job. I was shocked when he told me that nobody—nobody!—had gotten the simple answer correct. But then our discussion went to the next step, to contemplate what unintended consequences could come from using only that simple measure. Were the jobs paying enough to supplant the cash benefits? Were participants facing issues with childcare availability or affordability that forced them out of the program entirely but kept them in financial crisis? Should we look at a few measures to ensure that we don't drive those unintended consequences by measuring only one outcome that could therefore be gamed?

The outcomes may also be difficult or even impossible to measure, but we can usually find some proxy measures (often multiple output measures combined) to allow us some insight as to whether we're getting to the outcomes we want. In the long run, I really don't much care how we get to those outcomes, as long as we are staying solidly within the rules, and we get there in a way that doesn't drive unintended consequences. We must always keep our eye on the outcome(s) we're driving toward as our "true north."

DOCUMENT, DOCUMENT, DOCUMENT (AND THEN DOCUMENT SOME MORE)

After you've found a way to challenge the rules, document what you've done. A note to the file, an email to yourself, an email to someone else; it doesn't have to be formal or time intensive to be helpful. File it in a way that you can find it later. I promise you, as creative as you are on this and as much as you think you'll remember your reasoning in the future, you likely won't. Even if you do, you won't remember the legal citations you used. And those citations may change over time, so you want a record from when you made the determination. This is most critical in compliance-heavy industries, but I'd argue that it is critical even in the least compliance-heavy ones. First, there are no industries in which actual rules don't apply. But even if you're not reviewing actual legal citations, you want to remember later how you've pushed boundaries and what your thinking was when you did.

While you don't need to be a lawyer, you should write up your documentation with as much detail as possible. Put the legal citations—the black-letter law, the case law, whatever you find—in there with links to the documents online, or copy and paste the relevant language (or, better yet, both). Write down your interpretations of that language and why you think you are correct in that interpretation. Write down what people told you about "the way things are done" and why you've decided to do things differently. This doesn't have to be time or labor intensive, unless you're really pushing legal precedent and need to be able to defend your decision. Even a few bullet points can help when questions arise later.

I cannot tell you how many times I've been grateful to have that documentation when a question comes up well after the decision is made. Sometimes it is because I need to reassure myself that I had the interpretation right—or check to see if the law has changed at all and therefore changed our ability to approach things the same way we had. Sometimes it is because someone else, someone with power to change our approach, asks us why we aren't doing things the way everyone else does it. In any case, being able to point back to an interpretation, particularly one that was saved to the file at the time, is always helpful.

There are very few times that documentation is not called for, and if you find yourself wondering if it would be problematic to document your decision, it probably should make you stop and wonder if you're doing the right thing. If you can't put it in writing, it might be something you shouldn't do. Documentation isn't just helpful when you are pushing on the rules—to be clear, you should be documenting any decision that has potential risk involved, even if you are staying solidly in the standards rather than pushing into any gray areas.

That said, you should be extremely careful about *how* you document anything; I've always used the "*Washington Post* test" as our standard. If it isn't going to play well on the front page of the *Washington Post*, don't put it in writing.

That means you need to watch what you're saying in text, in email, and in any notes or other documentation you save. We all tend to be casual in texts and emails because we aren't often thinking about anyone else being able to read them. But there is very little in this world now that is truly private; someone can easily hack into your systems, or you may eventually be subject to legal discovery. Or, as we probably all have done at some point, you could send it to the wrong person. One person I knew routinely sent something to the wrong text thread. Sometimes it was funny or maybe a bit cringeworthy. One time she texted her husband to complain about her boss but sent the text to her boss instead. Oops. Awkward but manageable. But a couple of times it made things very challenging because the wrong person saw something they really shouldn't have.

Assume everything you put into writing could be discovered at some point. Would it be hard to explain? Could it be taken out of context? Could it blow up an important relationship?

You absolutely must be able to have hard conversations openly with your colleagues and trusted advisors. But particularly sensitive issues are much better in person or on the phone rather than in writing. You can, and likely should, reduce that conversation to written documentation later—but with carefully chosen words that support your decision, rather than showing the open and honest sausage making. In those cases, those open conversations aren't (hopefully) raising a red flag that you're doing the wrong thing but that you are hashing through big, hairy issues. If you can still reduce the decision to something you are comfortable putting in writing, you're likely on the right path. Once we have mastered the rules—those that are written and those that are unwritten—we can really start to get Unruly by finding that space within the rules where we can distinguish ourselves, pursue our chosen path, and forge our authentic version of breakout success.

5

REVEAL YOUR SUPERPOWER

One of my favorite shows as a kid was *The Greatest American Hero*, where an ordinary guy gets superpowers when wearing a superhero suit given to him by aliens. Unfortunately, he loses the instruction manual, so has to learn about his superpowers through trial and error. He not only has to figure out what those superpowers are, but how best to incorporate them into his superhero ways to fight crime and injustice.

If we can be like the *Greatest American Hero* and explore our own superpowers, we can leverage them not for hilarious crime fighting but for supercharged success. Understanding your superpowers can help to determine your differentiator—although they aren't always exactly the same thing—and thereby create a force for next-level outcomes. But how can our everyday actions lead us to figure out what our superpowers are and how to best use them?

Over the years in our company, we talked a lot about employees' leading and trailing edges. "Leading edge" is a term often applied to technology—to mean something that represents the most advanced or innovative aspects of a field. Something that is leading edge is on the forefront or vanguard.

As we relate it to people, our leading edges are things that either come easily to us or that we have acquired, usually through hard work, and turned into something we excel in. In contrast, a trailing edge is something that, for whatever reason, we struggle to perform well. The key is in identifying and naming these leading and trailing edges, from the perspectives of employees and across the hierarchical chain. While introspection is critical, I've found that getting some outside perspective is necessary to gain clarity in identifying unrecognized leading edges along with the trailing edges we may be overlooking.

In using leading and trailing edges, it is important that you do work that pushes you out of your comfort zone to actively develop trailing edges that are critical skills in your chosen domain. In the company, as we structured people's roles, we balanced a large portion of their portfolio in their leading-edge space, where we knew that they could easily and naturally succeed, but we'd also look for growth opportunities to push in their trailing edges, so that they were always building beyond where they were comfortable.

It is not groundbreaking to recognize that specific weaknesses may hold you back in career progression, or that you should identify your core strengths and pursue a career trajectory that builds upon them. But strengths and weaknesses look at things from a traditional perspective—what are the standard traits for a role and how do you fit or not fit those traits? But by looking at leading and trailing edges, rather than strengths and weaknesses, we can look at our core traits from an Unruly perspective and figure out how to place our authentic self in the best position to meet the outcomes we want. We can determine how to turn those trailing edges that are holding us back into authentic leading edges, or we can pivot away from those trailing edges to embrace our own superpowers rather than the ones that "everyone" who is successful in that realm seems to have. Not surprisingly, I'm *not* a big believer that you must fit the standard mold to find success in specific roles; but you *do* have to understand what the metrics of success are and figure out how you can meet them your own way, if you're not going to meet them in the traditional way.

If you do realize that the path you're on is no longer the right fit for you, a deep dive into your current leading and trailing edges can also help guide you to a new career trajectory. We can make the Unruly decision that we don't want to pursue something that "everyone" says is the right path if it doesn't match our leading and trailing edges, and we can't effectively modify a trailing edge to allow us to be successful. I've particularly seen this in people who feel like they "should" get into a specific role because it is more prestigious or more lucrative, and this exercise in looking objectively at leading or trailing edges can help determine if and how they can and should pursue that. It can also guide us when a role had been a great fit previously, but either that role morphs over time or we have grown over time; we can use a closer look at our leading and trailing edges to show us where we might want to pivot.

Let me give you an example of someone in our firm who fully embraced the leading and trailing edges concept over the course of her long tenure with us. Jennifer came to us in Italy as an analyst, after a professional career in financial management that had been significantly interrupted by her spouse's military moves. Her technical skills in financial management were superb, and she would have easily been much more senior in her career before she came to us but was affected by having to leave each job just as she was up for a well-deserved promotion. We all identified her technical skills as one of her leading edges, and we soon realized that another leading edge was the comfort she gave to our customers because of her quiet and trustworthy demeanor. She identified her introversion and low confidence as her trailing edges. She felt both were holding her back in moving into a leadership role. We also identified together that, while her math skills were top-notch, her writing skills were also a trailing edge.

But as she developed in her role in Italy and took on a role as the site lead, we all started realizing that her introversion was propelling one of her leading edges—her ability to engender trust and comfort with customers. She started organically driving some of our business development—our sales—because she *didn't* seem so sales-y. She certainly also gained confidence by doing progressively harder and more high-level work, but when she consistently kept humble and didn't project over-confidence, her demeanor also became a leading rather than a trailing edge. We realized that she did incredibly well in a role where she could develop long-term relationships based on her leading edges. As long as she stayed in a role that played to those leading edges and didn't rely too much on the more traditional business-development skills (particularly the ability to write well, which never became a leading edge), she was incredibly successful.

But as the company grew, and our roles got more specialized, she took on roles that were entirely focused on business development. In those roles, the skill sets we needed from her became misaligned with her leading and trailing edges. As a result, she eventually left our firm to join a smaller firm that needed her organic business-development and program-management skills to continue to succeed based on her authentic talents.

WHAT'S SO SPECIAL ABOUT YOU?

Beyond leading and trailing edges, I find it helpful to focus on one or two superpowers that each of us uniquely have. A superpower is a broad-based ability that amalgamizes a number of leading edges into a global force for that person. Probably my biggest superpower, outside of my overall ability to forge nontransactional relationships quickly and effectively, is my ability to see the hybrid solution that nobody else sees. This takes a number of my leading edges—my rational optimism that allows me to find a reasonable path to "yes" to mitigate risks and truly deliver; my ability to turn any "no" into a motivator; and my knowledge of (or ability to find) the rules and interpret them effectively to clear a new path—and coalesces them into the superpower that has driven so much of my individual and our company successes. This power of yes and power of no is, in combination with grit and wit to plow through the roadblocks, the centerpiece of my ability to achieve breakout success.

My colleague Heidi has a people-centric superpower that drove much of our success in creating our remarkably strong culture—but also in navigating difficult situations and mitigating our risk in doing so. She has a way of driving strong, collaborative relationships between people, which helped to create our strong culture of support. She also had what we called "the butter"—where she could manage any fraught communication with perfect tone and pitch. Heidi was amazing at keeping people calm and engaged in tense situations—by recognizing how each person's motivations could contribute to a balanced solution. I've personally seen her, multiple times, navigate a complicated employee termination, where things could have easily gone sideways. Instead, through empathy and perspective, the employee ends up thanking her for giving them the opportunity to grow elsewhere. This superpower came from some clear leading edges. For one, she has an innate calm and empathy in difficult situations. She can read people and recognize how their own personalities would interact well and poorly with other personalities in the group. She also has a foundational understanding that people, if treated with dignity over time in their workplace, want to partner in finding solutions even in difficult situations. These microinvestments build trust, and when trust is foundational in a workplace, business can be put first because people know they are a part of the business and not simply tools used to drive business. She also had a way of speaking that was precise but warm and organic and fully authentic, so she got her messages across carefully without looking too curated. And while she genuinely cared deeply about people, she was also stellar in holding reasonable boundaries effectively without making people feel rejected or defensive.

How do you determine your own superpower(s)? Well, just like with leading and trailing edges, it takes both introspection and an external perspective. One of the ways we used to help define people's superpowers was to ask the question: "What is your highest and best use?" In other words, where can you be most effective? This isn't necessarily just what you're best at but what you're best at *that is meaningful to the outcome* you're trying to achieve. What things can you do that will differentiate you from everyone else in the arena you're trying to play in? How do your leading and trailing edges come together with your goals and aspirations to create a force field of your own personal superpowers?

Think of it this way: If you are a professional football player, you are probably in top physical shape, and you are likely better than anyone else around you who isn't an athlete at anything physical. You're probably really good at mowing the lawn with a push mower, and you're likely much more effective at it than the neighborhood kid you could hire to do the work. You *could* do it faster and better than the neighbor kid, but your time is much better spent on the thing you can do better than anyone else that gets you to where you want to be, which is to be a more competitive, higher performing football player. That's your highest and best use, and that will help define your superpower.

But what makes this exercise an Unruly one is to look

outside what a traditional strengths-and-weaknesses exercise might give you. You need to be creative, like Jennifer was in her original leading- and trailing-edge review. She recognized that her introversion and her credibility in long-standing relationships gave her an advantage in certain types of sales because she was so untraditional in her approach. Her superpower was her stealth sales skills. If she had done a traditional review of her strengths and weaknesses, she would have entirely missed that as a superpower and stayed away from all business development. As it was, she was great at a particular type of sales, and she was even more successful than traditional sales professionals when she played to that superpower.

THE POWER OF YES

So much of our company success came from just saying yes and then figuring it out and making it happen. It was, bluntly, a Get $h!t Done mentality. But the critical piece was "and then making it happen," not just "saying yes." How did we make it happen? There was certainly a part of it that was just working hard—harder than I'd ever worked before—but it was much more about finding alternate paths and plotting them out clearly in a way that allowed us to execute to a desired outcome. We knew we couldn't fail, and so we put in the work to make sure we didn't fail. It was hard work, sure, but hard work alone wouldn't have gotten us there. It was a systematic look through all of the things that were standing in our way and figuring out a way around them. The power of yes, if you can live it, can be a universal superpower.

The power of yes takes four elements:

1. Putting in the work to build ownership in your career.
2. Embracing rational optimism.
3. Finding or creating the path to delivering what you promise.
4. Spoon-feeding solutions to those who lack a Get $h!t Done mentality.

Own Your Career

One of the hardest things about being an entrepreneur is that you own everything—the wins, the losses, the risk, the work. Particularly in the early years, most entrepreneurs spend all day working *in* the business and then most of the night working *on* the business. I know that, for me in those early years, I didn't get much more than four hours of sleep most nights. There's no guarantee that you'll get the reward, even if you put in the work and do everything right, but in the end, you have the ownership of whatever you've built. It is easy to "own" your career when you have ownership or equity in the business.

But even if you're not an entrepreneur with your own company, you can "own" your career and your career trajectory and build equity in your career rather than your company. It is less risky to work for someone else than to entirely strike out on your own; the entrepreneurial path provides that high risk but potentially higher reward. But in taking an entrepreneurial view of your career, you can take calculated risks of your own while on your path and balance the risk and reward you want.

In sales, we talk about your "book of business"—the

opportunities and relationships you own and can take with you from place to place. A book of business generally refers to which customers you have strong relationships with that can translate to sales revenue, but you don't have to be in sales to identify your book of business (or, if you'd rather think of it in a broader way, your book of opportunities and knowledge). Your book of business takes your leading and trailing edges, your superpowers, and your relationships, and it translates that whole package into actionable meaning to your employer. That book of business is critical to cultivate, regardless of whether you are an owner or an employee. In fact, it is just as critical as an employee in proving your worth to your current and prospective employers: being able to verbalize what that book of business looks like will be key to career progression.

You don't have to stay in the same type of role to bring along a book of business; you can absolutely pivot and still bring skills and relationships to a new role. The key is to identify what you're bringing to a role that not only differentiates you from others but yields meaningful outcomes. One of my friends, Liz, pivoted from a set of Division 1 college basketball head coaching positions to run a nonprofit focused on military spouse employment. Let me tell you, she knew better than anyone how to motivate people to get the work done, she knew how to lead a team, and she knew how to manage donors and other stakeholders. Plus, she brought entirely new relationships to a space that had been a fairly closed circuit, which opened up new options for donors, for employers, and for mentors and advocates well beyond those who had been traditionally participating when she started.

Embracing Rational Optimism

If you can't tell by now, I believe that most success in every realm comes in the gray areas between extremes. This is definitely critical in the balance between optimism and pessimism, where you find the equilibrium between bravado and paralysis. You're seeking a balance that's unique to you, but finding a path away from either extreme is key to breakout success.

There's pretty overwhelming research that optimism provides better outcomes than pessimism on almost every measure. So certainly, based on the research, it is useful to tip the balance toward optimism—but not unfettered optimism. Over the years, I've thought of the balanced middle as "rational optimism." There are other people who have used the term differently—many different people, all with different definitions of the phrase—but what I mean is simply that we do the work to balance between the idea that the sky is falling and the belief that everything will always work out in the end. Rational optimism allows us to know, and try to mitigate, almost all the things that can go wrong, but to remain optimistic about our ability to navigate to a positive outcome.

Plenty of people are naïve optimists; they believe they can do anything and everything, and they think that sheer force of will or hard work (or a pretty face and sunny disposition) can get them there. That method is sure to run them off a cliff at some point, because they haven't planned enough to be able to manage everything that could go wrong. Often, these are the folks who later become disillusioned and think the deck is stacked against them because they couldn't succeed in anything they ever tried—but that's because they never did the real work of plotting out the path and the pitfalls.

But on the flip side, there are plenty of people who are also smart and hardworking but always see so much danger around every corner that they become incapacitated and can't take risks; they become paralyzed with the fear of failure. I've seen a whole lot of these folks go to law school, for good reason. The best lawyers can see every risk, no matter how unlikely it may be in the real world. But the less skilled of them don't temper that fear with a calculation of how likely the disaster might be and what they're giving up to avoid the potential disaster.

This isn't to say that these people are wrong in their assessments of what can go awry—they are often realists who can identify actual risks and help mitigate them. When not taken to the extreme, these pessimists can be incredibly adept at managing these risks and keeping the perennial optimists from diving headfirst off a cliff. Saying yes without understanding risks and looking for ways to manage them is irresponsible. Saying no because of the potential for failure is paralyzing. As with any extreme, finding the balance is where the magic happens. The worst lawyers I've seen always find a way to say no to every new option. The best ones will find a way to say yes and mitigate as much as possible so that the risks are manageable.

We found that balance in rational optimism through a team approach in the firm. We had some senior leaders who saw every possible potential danger in every interaction, but they also could help negotiate around those dangers with brilliant strategy and legalese. And then there were those of us—including me—who would run full-speed ahead into opportunities, with a nod to the risks but a solid belief that we could make it to the desired outcome. The combination of all of us was so much better than the sum of our parts. So many times, I'd run full-speed ahead to some amazing opportunity, with others running after me, yelling, "Hold on, let's think about this!" By ourselves, some of us were rational optimists, emphasis on the *optimist*. Others were rational optimists, emphasis on the *rational*. Between all of us, we played in the middle of the rational optimist scale and leveraged it to our great advantage.

Finding the Path to Deliver What You Promised

As we were starting out, we kept our offerings to what I knew I could directly oversee—and, frankly, what I could jump in and take over if I had to. We only went away from my own core competencies once we built a strong enough team with a layer of oversight that could, themselves, jump in and manage things if anything went off the rails. Even now, we maintain control of our execution with the ability for senior leaders to oversee and even execute when necessary. It has been useful more times than I could easily count that we can tell a client when something goes wrong that they get the COO or even the CEO on their project to set things right. Failure wasn't an option, and we'd always make it right. It wasn't just that we said yes, but we said yes *and then delivered*.

That didn't mean that we weren't willing to stretch what we could in order to say yes anytime we could; we certainly took chances and went beyond what we'd done before. But in every case, we kept the delivery of our promises top of mind and made sure we had a path to deliver. You need to be able to *see* the barriers to be able to *plan for* the barriers to be able to *execute around* the barriers. And in the long run, when new barriers come up that you don't expect, you have to be able to *flex with* the new issues to find new solutions. You can't do any of that if you don't know the area well enough yourself or can't quickly and reliably obtain that knowledge. I am not a huge fan of the "burn your boat" analogy—that the only way to succeed is to take away your other options so you have to succeed—but if you're going to burn your boat, you'd better darn well know how to swim if things go wrong.

One company that truly exemplifies the power of yes overall, and particularly of finding the path to deliver even when you've stretched far beyond your comfort zone, is a firm started by a young military veteran named Mike, who had some experience in the GovCon industry when he decided to set out on his own. He had an impressive plan to blow right through the standard path of an emerging small business, and as he and I talked, I told him that I had some concerns about the ambitiousness of his plans, but that if anyone could do it, I knew it was him. He and his team went after a massive—almost half a billion dollar—competition against all the large standard-bearer tech firms where there would be one winner only. As a brand-new and tiny business, his team beat out the large, established businesses, including one of the largest defense contractors who had been performing the work to date. But then this tiny firm had to deliver—and they did. Mike and his team knew the work and jumped in to manage it, regardless of how small they were and how large the project was. From that, they grew to a large business that could effectively compete with the "big boys" in all sorts of arenas, because they already proved they could do it. The power of yes in action.

Do Others' Homework for Them

Most people don't have an Unruly mentality; they look for the path of least resistance whenever they can. That's why it is so imperative never to take the first no answer as a definitive. But we can use this basic fact to our Unruly advantage—by doing their homework for them.

We've talked a lot about how time-intensive the Unruly path can be. It takes substantial research and coordination to learn the rules well. It takes even more effort to find the way to the yes answer within the rules. Most people aren't willing to do that work. They take the easy answer they think is right—and fast—and leave it at that. They believe the baseline of what they were taught originally, and they never go back to the source documentation. If their old boss told them something twenty years ago, that's what they are going to continue to do.

That approach serves most people very well if they're not looking for breakout success, if they just want to fly under the radar and get their work done. It also serves people well when they're trying to conserve energy. Nobody can take the Unruly approach to every single thing in life every single time. We'll talk more in chapter 8 about when it makes sense to stop pushing so hard. It is truly how most people approach work, and it works for them, and that's perfectly fine.

In the cases where we want to push through a "no" answer, though, we can make it easy for them to say yes by doing the Unruly homework for them. Show them your Unruly research about what the rules actually say, but do it in a way that is easily digestible for them. Anticipate any questions or concerns they may have and be ready with answers to those questions and documentation to show why your answer works. I will often prepare—usually not for distribution, but for my own reference—a question and answer (Q&A) document to keep handy when we're trying to take an Unruly path to upend something, so that we can be ready to respond with prepared, smart, knowledgeable answers. You will have more influence by being prepared in the moment rather than relying on another's willingness to revisit an issue or pertinent fact.

Make it easier for them to say yes than to say no. And if they do say no, politely provide a path to get them to yes. Remember your two-year-old's questions and keep asking until they just say yes because it is way too hard to keep saying no.

THE POWER OF NO

I always say that the four most powerful words that drove my success are: *Oh, really? Watch me.* My team would consistently joke that the way to get me to do anything was to tell me that someone said I couldn't do it. The instant someone put up a barrier in my way—or said somehow that *I* wouldn't be able to do something, or even that *anyone* couldn't do something—it would become a singular focus for me to prove them wrong. More than anything else, this was the defining trajectory of my success. Tell me I can't do something, and I'll prove you wrong, damn it.

So many people hear no and simply shut down. Others get energized by no and want to prove everyone wrong. If you have the tendency to shut down, what are some basic techniques to translate that no into action, rather than inertia?

One technique is to **take each action incrementally**; don't look at the entire big, hairy audacious thing you have to do but take it one step at a time. At each stage, you can make deals with yourself that you can just get through this phase, or that project, or to this outcome, and then you can quit if you still want to. At each step, promise yourself that you can quit at the next step, *but you won't quit right then.* That one-step-at-a-time mentality served me well in getting through pretty much every challenge in my life, not just in my professional world. How do you eat an elephant? One bite at a time.

We recently had my daughter's teammate and her mom staying with us for a hockey tournament, and they got a call one morning saying that the girl's father had unexpectedly passed away. The mom was, understandably, completely overwhelmed, and she kept saying she wasn't sure how she was going to handle everything without her husband. I helped her take care of the immediate logistics of the next twenty-four hours (getting home, getting people there to help her son navigate everything, etc.), and I set a mantra for her and her daughter: "We just have to get through the next five minutes. I can get through the next five minutes." That incremental approach, particularly to something that is truly overwhelming, can be a game changer.

I absolutely love the quote: "Those who say it cannot be

done should not interrupt those who are doing it." Recognize that the naysayers often have their own agenda for telling you that you can't do something. And honestly, they're right in thinking *they* can't do something. They just don't know if *you* can do it or not. Often, they're so invested in thinking something can't be done, because it's a way to save their own ego—since they can't do it, it can't possibly be done.

Rational optimism is also critical here. When someone tells you that you can't do something, ask the two-year-old's question: *Why not?* If there's a good reason you can't do it right now, what can you do to make it possible in short order—or later? What are the barriers, and how do you bust through those barriers? If you take that rational optimism approach where you identify the barriers and risks and determine if it actually is possible, you can navigate yourself to the "Oh, really, watch me" mentality.

The combination of being **witty and gritty** can also help you utilize the power of no. Humor and grit go hand in hand—as shown consistently in both the research literature and in everyday life. Humor promotes feelings of well-being, optimism, feelings of control, and self-efficacy, and it decreases negative thinking, stress, depression, and anxiety. Grit requires courage, conscientiousness, perseverance, resilience, and passion. In any stressful situation where grit is required, humor can lay the groundwork for that ability to persevere. Laughing cuts the tension and gives us the willpower to push through the hardest of times.

One of the "founding stories" of WWC is when a no turned into a doubling of the firm in twenty-four hours. Our first contract was, as I recounted earlier, overseeing business case analyses for the regional Anti-Terrorism/Force Protection office. I had no idea about anything related to AT/FP, including that AT/FP stood for Anti-Terrorism/Force Protection. But my customer, our Saint Tony, told me that he needed someone good at analytics, and he would help guide me through the specifics on AT/FP.

Tony and I were set to travel to DC about six months into that first contract to brief the DC-based headquarters command that was paying for my contract. Tony got called away to brief the four-star admiral at the last minute, and he was very concerned about me going to DC by myself. I confidently told him that I could handle myself—after all, I had gone up against cabinet-level secretaries in my OMB job. He told me that the senior civilian in the office was "difficult," but again I brushed him off and said I'd dealt with difficult people my whole life and would be fine.

I got to DC and sequentially briefed everyone on the AT/FP staff over the course of my weeklong trip. Late Thursday afternoon of that week, I finally walked into the office of the senior civilian, the "difficult client" that Tony was so worried about. He was a recently retired Navy Commander who was now a government civilian. He told me to close the door behind me, and I didn't get my name out of my mouth before he started berating me loudly and with lots of four-letter words. He spent the better part of two hours calling me stupid and telling me that he was going to cancel my contract. I stayed calm and just tried to focus on the content of his concerns rather than his delivery. When he couldn't get a rise out of me by telling me he'd cancel my contract, he told me that he expected me to move back to DC full-time to work directly for him. I told him that, respectfully, if I was going to move back to DC, it would be for one of the three senior executive jobs I had offers for (those jobs being multiple levels above the job he was filling at that point), and that I was happy to travel back frequently, but that I had moved to Europe and would be staying there with my husband. If that wasn't what he wanted, he was welcome to cancel the contract any time. With that, he yelled at me that he *wasn't* going to cancel my contract but that he was instead adding two people to it (this was supposed to be bad?!). He expected me to hire someone else in Italy and someone in Bahrain in short order, although he made clear that he thought I couldn't pull it off. With that, he sent me out of his office and told me to be back Friday morning and to stay an extra week in DC.

I went back to the hotel—steaming mad, mind you, but without ever letting him see that he had gotten to me—and started making phone calls. I stayed up until midnight, which was 6 AM Naples time, to call my husband and some friends on base to see if they could help me find someone in Naples and someone in Bahrain. I went to bed for a few hours, and by the time I woke up at 3 or 4 AM, my friend Jayme had a military spouse in Naples who was absolutely perfect, and my husband had the phone number of a retired Navy Commander who had stayed in Bahrain after his recent retirement and was looking for a job. I interviewed both Megan and Eric that morning, and when I walked into the office at 7 AM, I had two stellar resumes of people who were willing to start immediately. The customer tried to find something wrong with both of them, but they were each ideal, and he had to admit defeat and begrudg-ingly give me kudos for staffing two overseas positions within twelve hours (overnight!!!). I love this story, because it wraps up so much of the Unruly mindset: the power of yes, the power of no, the power of your village, and the power of rational opti-mism. And it was the catalyst for initial growth that took the company to a feasible path to sustainability and diversification.

6

WHAT'S THE WORST THAT CAN HAPPEN, CHICKEN LITTLE?

Too many leaders are constantly looking around for what can go wrong and framing everything as a catastrophe. There is obviously wisdom in business and leadership for knowing what can possibly go awry and planning for it. But if you turn into Chicken Little, constantly claiming that the sky is falling, you will become paralyzed, and you will paralyze (and exhaust) everyone around you. Always looking for the perfect [whatever] will stop progress in its tracks. Nothing will ever be perfect, and the drive to perfection will stop you from achieving anything.

For these Chicken Littles, there is often no distinction between slight inconveniences and the truly catastrophic problems—and when every problem is equally awful, no progress can be made to work through any part of the problem. They simply cannot say yes when presented with an opportunity, because they can't get past everything that could go wrong.

NOT MAKING A DECISION IS A DECISION

Chicken Little thinking can lead to inertia. I have seen so many leaders get overwhelmed by the amount of data they can gather or feel like they should gather. Look, I'm a data geek. I am a huge believer in making decisions based on real, good-quality, actionable data. But you will never have perfect data, and you will never have it fast enough to make all your decisions, particularly the smaller everyday decisions. Paralysis by analysis is a very real phenomenon. I've seen way too many people fail to take advantage of an opportunity because they simply do not make a decision quickly enough. Sometimes, the inability to decide is because of the downward spiral of pessimism, but there are plenty of other reasons that people get stuck and just defer a decision.

If you postpone a decision, often you're essentially making a decision in so doing. You lose the ability to make the decision in that delay. That's a huge problem if that's not what you want to do. Obviously, many leaders are terrified by this decision-making process because they fear making the wrong decision. Here's the thing. There are very few decisions that can't be walked back. Certainly, there's some cost to walking back decisions, but there are generally larger costs of not making any decision in the first place. And there are ways to start down a path but put in controls or touch points to make sure that you continue to be confident in that decision so that you can change course quickly and effectively if needed.

I feel like so many leaders are so worried that they're going to make the sky fall by making the wrong decision that they end up actually making the sky fall as a result of the delay. So, let's look at ways we can get around our Chicken Little brain and into productive decision-making and action.

REWIRING YOUR PESSIMISTIC BRAIN

As I've told you, I am, at my core, an optimist. I'm not sure I was born as one—anxiety is genetically my default—but my parents definitely trained it into me from an early age. First and foremost, they truly believed that I could do almost anything I set my mind to. Except singing. They knew I couldn't sing and reminded me of that every time I tried.

Pretty much everything else, they truly believed I could do, but here's the trick—they didn't just believe I could, they gave me the tools I needed to do it well rather than just blowing smoke. They gave me honest feedback so that I could get better. They coupled unconditional love and support with meaningful resources and a push to continuously grow. In other words, while they believed I *could* do anything I set my mind to, they showed me that I still had to work for it and make it happen. As importantly, they also taught me not to let setbacks shut me down or force me to quit, so that I could stay generally optimistic in my overall expectations for eventual success. Roadblocks may slow you down, but there's always a way around them.

But I also grew up as a kid in a post-Holocaust world in a Russian/Lithuanian Jewish family that, for centuries, moved all over Eastern Europe to escape regular pogroms, and that generational trauma is embedded in our DNA and drives existential anxiety for every single person in my family. The dread that something could and likely will go wrong was always just below the surface. Show those of us with anxiety any overall-positive situation, and our minds will generate a couple dozen ways—from likely to almost-but-not-quite impossible—that things can go awry.

These competing tendencies of optimism and anxiety are a perfect combination for breakout success in business and in life. Optimism helps us believe we can get $h!t done with grit and hard work, but anxiety lets us see, and address, all of the places where things might go wrong. This is where my parents had it exactly right. They taught me that I had to put in the work and figure out how to do it, not just that it would magically appear from on high. As we talked about in the last chapter, this rational optimism is key to producing a productive balance between Pollyanna and Chicken Little.

There is significant research that shows that optimists (and particularly rational optimists) far outperform pessimists on pretty much every aspect in life—from financial and career success to relationship success to physical health to happiness. Basically, pessimists generally may be correct in their assessments of the world, but research over multiple domains consistently shows that optimists allow for better outcomes and, in the long run, reach them more effectively. The good news is: we have strong evidence, from the research of

Martin Seligman and others, that while people are generally coded to be more or less optimistic by genetics or early-life circumstances, pessimism and optimism can also be learned, and with effort, even the most extreme pessimist can become more optimistic.

One of the reasons that pessimism is so detrimental is because it stops you before you ever start. Pessimists often use their outlook to opt out entirely and stop trying to succeed because they know they can't. It becomes a vicious cycle. They believe they can't succeed, so they don't try, and then they don't succeed and prove their pessimistic outlook. It is much easier to just tell yourself that there's no reason to do something hard because it won't work than it is to try it and see if it works. Sometimes, it seems that people in this mindset are more comfortable in failure than in success. Either way, if you try or you don't try for something hard, you might encounter failure. But only when you attempt it do you have the *option* for success. Bottom line—if you believe you can or you believe you can't, either way you're right. So which way would you rather live your life?

Cognitive behavioral therapy (CBT) is one of the most powerful tools in clinical psychology, and I have used it throughout my own life and as a leader entirely outside of the mental health field. It is one of the best ways to move you forward toward rational optimism. The core underpinnings of it are useful for your own thought processes but can also help you guide others—employees, outside partners, competitors, even your children—oftentimes without having to call out the fact that you're using CBT techniques.

Challenging Cognitive Distortions

At its most basic, CBT is a reality-testing paradigm that can bring you more in line with realistic optimism. The central tenet of CBT is challenging cognitive distortions (incorrect thoughts) to help regulate emotions and develop positive coping strategies for everyday life stressors. It is not the "tell me about your childhood" type of psychotherapy, but it provides tools that anyone can use to test their own view of the world and shift their perspective to be more effective for living a happy and productive life. At its core, CBT tools help you reframe your thoughts to get to the outcomes you desire, which seems minor but really gets to the core of rational optimism. By changing the way you perceive a situation, you can change your reactions to that situation and therefore the actions you take to manage or mitigate any situation.

Using the tools of CBT, I tend to ask myself one major question—with two additional follow-up questions—when faced with a big decision or a negative thought. *What is the worst thing that could happen?* This can be a great exercise for a pessimist—they get to let their brain run wild with the catastrophes that could befall them—but *then* it is time to unpack that thought.

Sure, you could make the wrong decision in taking on an opportunity that is outside of your comfort zone, and you could fail. But what next? If the cascade of thoughts takes you down the road to the idea that failure on this one project will mean losing all credibility in your industry and being fired and never getting hired anywhere else and losing your home and becoming homeless and turning to drugs and . . . and . . .

and . . . you need to take the next step in this CBT journey. *How likely are any of these things to happen?* Maybe the first catastrophe is somewhat likely. How likely is the next terrible descent into doom even if the first one happens? And the next one after that, and after that? When you start multiplying the probability of each unlikely (but possible) outcome together, the odds of the truly catastrophic end are infinitesimal. But hold on, we're not done yet.

The last step is a second follow-on question: *How can I mitigate the risks of everything that could go wrong?* Even with infinitesimal risks, and certainly with likely risks, there may be a way to make sure that they are less likely or less catastrophic if they happen. Can you take additional steps to ensure that the first catastrophic thing doesn't happen—or apply failsafe measures to the next one after that? Can you set break points where if two or three negative things happen in succession, and the truly catastrophic thing now could happen, you stop and pursue a different path, regardless of how much time and energy you've already expended? If there is a likely bad outcome with no way to mitigate the risk, even if the upside is significant, it may not be the right path for you to take (depending on your own risk tolerance and the expected return on investment, or ROI). If you can't put a plan in place to lessen the likelihood of the cavalcade of crisis from taking over—if there are no guardrails you can put up to get off the ride if and when it starts moving down the crisis path, it may not be worth it.

If you are operating within a realistic optimism mindset, this exercise might become less emotionally fraught, because it seems like second nature, but the "realistic" part of the optimism means you still *should* run through the exercise to figure out what could go wrong. This exercise isn't meant to convince you that everything is a good idea but to control the anxiety of *distorted* thoughts and help mitigate the *real* threats. The secret to being able to say yes, even in the face of the catastrophe cavalcade, is to find the risks, quantify them, mitigate them to the extent possible, and then decide if the potential risk is worth the potential reward. It isn't always saying yes—Pollyanna doesn't work in the real world—but it certainly isn't saying no to avoid all risk. It also isn't doubling down when something goes wrong, because the next thing is unlikely to go wrong— this should be an ongoing risk/reward review at each phase so that you can pull out when you are starting to move toward a bad outcome.

Ever heard R.E.M.'s song, "It's the End of the World as We Know It (and I Feel Fine)"? This is the rational optimist's anthem. According to urban legend, at least in the high school debate world, it is about a high school debate tournament, and the tendency of arguments in debate teams to take us down a catastrophe cavalcade. If you've ever seen a high school debate (at least during the late 1980s when the song was released), the winning team ends the argument by showing how their opponent's approach would inevitably yield nuclear war. Every single debate ended in total annihilation. But imagine if we could apply CBT. Essentially, that's what Michael Stipe did when he said it is the end of the world as we know it, *and I feel fine.*

Reframing

Another lesson from CBT is to reframe what looks to be a negative situation—to ask if you can possibly see it differently.

I use this all the time to defuse situations at work and particularly with teenagers at home. When someone says something—anything—that you believe is negative, stop and ask if it could be interpreted any other way. *Even if the most likely interpretation is that they meant it to be negative,* finding a different interpretation can be incredibly powerful for your own mental health, if nothing else. I use this with my daughter during the teenage-girl drama that constantly seems to swirl around female friendships at that age. Her friend will say something in a text, or post something on social media, that she immediately assumes is an attack on her. Once she has the headspace to look rationally at the situation, we'll explore if it could possibly be interpreted a different way. Many times, it can, and we talk about if she can possibly start with the assumption that they meant well instead. Of course, there are some cases where someone *isn't* a good friend and *shouldn't* be given the benefit of the doubt (particularly after multiple chances), but at least if we start with the expectation of good intentions, we've got a good grounding for the rest.

It works particularly well when someone is being snarky or sarcastic, or even if they're just letting off steam. One of my favorite quotes comes from Ruth Bader Ginsburg's mother-in-law, on the eve of RBG's wedding. She said, "Sometimes it pays to be a little deaf." Ignoring certain things is crucial for relationship preservation. My husband has a funny habit of muttering when he's annoyed. He doesn't say anything *to* any of us, but particularly when there's a mess in the kitchen or the hockey bags aren't aired out (if you know, you know), he mutters his displeasure. When we first got married, I'd confront him, and we'd end up arguing. And then at some point in our early years, I asked him how he'd like me to handle it when he was muttering, and he said he didn't mean anything by it, it was just his way of blowing off steam, and he just wanted to be left alone. So, now I know to just let him mutter.

Psychological Safety

The concept of psychological safety is critical for taking the risks necessary in rational optimism. I once had a boss who told us that he'd give us enough rope to hang ourselves, but if we screwed up, we'd be on our own. Luckily, *his* boss instead made clear that we'd have the backing to manage around mistakes and take risks without fear of reprisal. The first boss made it dangerous to take risks. The boss's boss gave us the space to do so. Without that space—that psychological safety—it would not be rational to be overly optimistic or to take any risks for outsize success. Without psychological safety, you rationally should be in a "duck and cover" mentality.

There is no doubt that when you're pushing outside of the standard ways of doing things, you're going to make mistakes and you're going to fail. That is what sets you up for the opportunities for breakout success. You, and those around you supporting you, are going to have to be comfortable with the idea that mistakes will happen and aren't fatal. Almost any mistake can be walked back, can be fixed, and might even lead to better outcomes in the end. But that only works when you've got the space, in your leadership's view and in your own brain, to take those chances while knowing you can manage any fallout.

So, it is critical to give yourself psychological safety to fail, and particularly if you are a leader, to give those around you psychological safety. That means being open to failure as a means to success.

Don't Tell Me About Your Mother

Beyond just CBT, I am a big believer in more traditional therapy—still not quite the "tell me about your mother" Freudian model, but the kind that allows you to understand your unconscious thoughts and biases, your own metacognitions (the thoughts about your thoughts), and the ways in which you consistently react that may be less than optimal. This self-reflection is paramount to effective leadership and strategy—and particularly to making sure you know your own moral compass and continue to follow it. Using an outside, professional observer to interact with, be it a therapist or coach, can't fully be reproduced by a friend or colleague in the same way, so I do think that everyone can benefit from initial therapy and regular "tune-ups" or check-ins with a supportive therapist or coach when you're facing a challenging situation.

While I'd strongly suggest that everyone seek out external help beyond their village or their kitchen cabinet, you can also borrow from some of the basic tenets of therapy to challenge your thoughts and actions or leverage your colleagues to help you do so. There are tons of more in-depth resources for doing intensive work along the optimism/pessimism continuum, as well, but in brief, a few tools:

- **Highlighting cognitive dissonance**: Where your thoughts and behaviors or two thoughts are in conflict, it can create a powerful drive to resolve them, called "cognitive dissonance," as we talked about in chapter 3. But if you don't keep your core beliefs central in your mind, it is easier to avoid cognitive dissonance because your behaviors aren't in conflict with the beliefs that are highlighted in your brain at that time. Something as simple as taping sayings to your computer screen or writing them on your office whiteboard or posting meaningful art on your walls can keep you from taking actions that are against your core beliefs without feeling the critical cognitive dissonance that can put you back on the right track.

- **Watch out for rumination**: Rumination, or the constant repetition of mistakes, problems, and negative emotions in your brain, can be a significant contributor to anxiety and depressive disorders, and it can increase the impact of the cognitive processing issues that come with these disorders. I talked earlier about the advice from my kids' favorite hockey coach to "be like Dory" (from *Finding Nemo*) and leverage short-term memory loss to move on from a mistake. Managing rumination isn't just a willpower issue, but if you find yourself fixated on problems beyond the immediate impact, and you can't seem to shift your focus, getting help to move beyond the tendency to ruminate will be critical for enhancing your ability to focus on new challenges.

- **Journaling (or verbal journaling)**: I know, journaling seems like the go-to method for making change these days, but everyone can benefit from documenting their thoughts effectively. There's some great research on why writing by hand is the most effective method, but there are plenty of reasons that some can't do that, and that's okay. Getting your thoughts out of your head any way that is comfortable for you is still effective. For me, I've found talk to text on my phone useful for verbal journaling. I've found the walk and talk, drive and talk, or even just pace and talk is my best bet—I get the physical energy out at the same time that I'm getting the emotional energy out, which does double duty.

- **Change your perspective**: Our cognitive perceptions can become fixed when our actual environment is fixed. When you need a change in attitude, or some clarity of focus, an actual change in perspective—a physical shift—can help a cognitive shift. When you're struggling, WALK AWAY. Not forever, but for a bit. The depth of the issue will likely drive the depth of the change you need, but even a ten-minute walk or a shift from one room to another can help.

- **Managing perfectionism**: The drive toward perfection can get in the way of the art of "good enough." With finite resources (particularly time and money), when an 80 percent solution is good enough, every extra minute or dollar that you spend on getting better than the 80 percent solution is a minute or a dollar you can't spend on something else. The marginal benefits of the extra money or time on the initial project pale in comparison to the marginal benefits you'd get from spending those dollars or minutes on a new project that you could also complete at 80 percent within the time it would take you to get close to the 100 percent solution on the first project. So, two good-enough projects, or one overly perfect project that didn't buy you much in terms of additional customer satisfaction or ongoing sales? Eighty percent—or 90 percent, or even 60 percent . . . whatever is good enough for that specific issue—is decidedly better if your resources can be put to better use elsewhere. But that takes getting comfortable in not being perfect and objectively asking yourself, "How good is good enough in this case?"

LESSONS IN MINDFULNESS

When we first got to Italy, the college on base asked me to teach a course in mindfulness, which was ironic because I've always been really bad at giving myself the cognitive space and calm that is central to mindfulness. I could teach the concepts well, but the practice of it has always been hard for me. I've tried over the years, and I've found that there are certain things that come naturally to me and other things that I just can't possibly master or will simply never feel comfortable with. As I've gotten older, I've realized that's okay. Mindfulness can easily be a choose-your-own adventure, where you can take from the menu of options that work for you and push the other techniques to the side. You might come back to them later, or never, but even if you only find one thing that works even slightly for you, that's progress, and progress begets more progress.

At its core, mindfulness is about creating space in your brain to respond to the environment on a higher level, rather than in the immediate moment in your reptilian brain. One of our closest friends is a rabbi who has become steeped in spiritual mindfulness, and I've learned a ton from him. And while he does weeklong silent retreats (which might actually kill me to attempt), he's also helped me to incorporate more of the techniques that didn't work for me when I was younger. Again, there are a ton of great resources out there around mindfulness, so I'm not going to go through the actual techniques here that can get you outside of your primal brain. Instead, I want to give you an understanding of what mindfulness can do for you if you want to explore it.

There's a way to conceive of mindfulness as layers of realization. **The first layer—the baseline marker of mindful awareness—can be used as an immediate stress-relieving technique.** Your sympathetic and parasympathetic nervous system and the fight-or-flight response (now more effectively thought of as fight/flight/freeze/fawn response) control your stress response. When faced with a stressor, your sympathetic nervous system kicks in and gets you ready for immediate action of some sort or another, which made sense in our Neanderthal days when stressors were things that could kill you immediately. Once the stressor has been dealt with—again, in Neanderthal days, that was almost immediate—your parasympathetic nervous system would kick in and clear out all the hormones and such that your sympathetic nervous system brought to the fight.

You can use a quick deep-breathing exercise to calm yourself in the moment of stress; just simple breathing in through your nose, holding your breath, and breathing out slowly through your mouth can work. But just note, I've had to learn to go on mute when I'm doing this on conference calls because people thought I was sighing in frustration, which was exactly the opposite effect I was going for! But that simple breath exercise gets you out of the immediate need to react and kicks in your parasympathetic nervous system when your stress-related sympathetic nervous system has taken over. You can manage that first layer with other techniques, like exercise or even specific tapping on pressure points to have the same effect. The first layer is all about the immediate response and trying to just give yourself time and space and change your nervous-system response in the moment.

The second layer of mindfulness is longer term and consists of using techniques to recognize and manage your thought patterns effectively. This thinking-about-thinking (called metacognition) is less in the moment and more about recognizing how your thoughts impact you across the board. This can come from meditation, where you recognize the thoughts that are crossing your mind and acknowledge and dismiss them or welcome them without judgment. Not to get too "woo-woo" here, but thoughts aren't *real*, they're ethereal. They only have the power we give to them.

A great example is food cravings, which are really just thoughts . . . albeit often *very* intrusive thoughts for many of us. Mindfulness can allow us to acknowledge those thoughts, accept them, and then choose how we want to act upon those thoughts. We can actively choose to eat to satisfy those cravings or not. The thought is just a thought. The action determines if we eat the whole batch of cookie dough in one sitting or not. We don't have to maintain control over our thoughts to be able to choose how we react to those thoughts. At least in concept. I'm still not very good at this one.

The next layer is to go beyond reacting to responding. At the core, the difference between these things is the thoughtful intention behind each. A reaction is unconscious; it happens *to* you automatically without thinking. A response is intentional; it happens *by* you with consciousness and purpose. Both reaction and response have a place in our repertoire. You want to be able to automatically react to a car braking in front of you, without the need for conscious thought and intention. But in most professional contexts, or even most personal ones, taking the time to determine how you will respond rather than react is critical. Once you can calm yourself in the first layer and start realizing how your thought patterns influence you, the next step is to take that pause, apply those lessons, and respond rather than react.

The final layer is getting entirely away from your logical side. My rabbi friend—who was a computer programmer before going to rabbinical school—calls this "hacking your brain," and I think that's a great description. While you're in a state of flow or tapping into your calmness or a different level of consciousness than you normally live in, you can plant seeds of other thoughts that get activated in your everyday brain. These can be thoughts of loving kindness, optimism, positive emotions—whatever you want.

From a neurological perspective, what you're doing in this is deepening the neural pathways (the brain connections) of the thoughts you want to strengthen and pruning back the pathways of the negative thoughts that hold you back. That's the hacking part—just like in a computer program, you're writing the code that makes things work in one way or another. Actively cultivating strong positive associations makes your brain more likely to default to those positive associations in the future. You change your brain by continuously and consciously forcing yourself into those positive pathways.

And while you can do this in the standard mindfulness techniques like meditation, if that isn't how you work effectively, there are other techniques that work as well. You can simply actively choose to find a specific number of positive things that happen every day and give gratitude for them. With that, you are starting to rewire your brain to identify the positive and discount the negative. If you turn that concept to your marriage, for example—and sit with your spouse for five minutes and simply tell them (and then have them tell you) all the things they are grateful for about you, without any negative caveats—you've rewired your relationship to be more positive. As you reinforce those neural networks in your brain repeatedly, it becomes a virtuous cycle.

You can use this for any thought you want to reinforce, not just optimism or gratitude. I have a colleague who asks his daughters routinely how they failed that day and celebrates their failures. He's reinforcing a risk-taking mentality for them, and his girls are expert at pushing themselves out of their comfort zones and finding outsize success in so doing, because they have an automatic predisposition for seeing failure as a natural and celebrated outcome of trying something hard.

NOT YOUR FATHER'S WAR GAMES

Our large Special Operations Command contract provides support to military training and exercise programs worldwide. On the most basic level, these exercises help our military "practice" going to war before they go off and fight. It allows them to face and learn how to manage potentially catastrophic situations without risk. There are all sorts of different exercises, from the very tactical boots-on-ground ones called "realistic military training" to much more strategic thought-based tabletop exercises. The latter include former senior leaders role-playing a military and diplomatic situation and injecting unexpected events throughout, so that the current military leaders can determine how they'd respond and what the follow-on consequences might be.

The idea of the exercises is to allow everyone to keep calm in the face of chaos, to get both the physical and mental muscle memory solid enough that some things that will regularly happen become second nature to handle. But you don't have to be a Navy SEAL to incorporate the concept into your own life. It doesn't have to be a formal or extravagant program—although some things within corporate life certainly can benefit from formally exercising a crisis, and some industries require it—but I find the less formal mental exercises are incredibly helpful in Chicken Little moments.

This can be as simple as a thought exercise, or you can increase the formality by thinking it through out loud to yourself or someone else or putting in place even more structure. Start where you are and mentally take the decision step you are thinking about taking. Play it out in your mind—what happens next? And then next after that? And next after that? And then, this part is critical: Back up and do it again. And again. Take different paths. Inject different situations. See how it plays out in different scenarios.

I also use this exercise technique to plan out difficult conversations, war-game big decisions, and plan out public remarks. I keep my phone near me (like pretty much everyone in the world at this point), and if I come up with a particularly inspired thought, I just use the notes function and talk to text to capture it. Or if I realize that I need to do something specific to mitigate a potential problem, I'll set a reminder on my phone and then move on so as not to interrupt my flow of thoughts.

IF IT WAS EASY, EVERYONE WOULD DO IT

Finally, just a simple reminder—something I tell myself constantly, as almost a mantra.

This is supposed to be hard. If it wasn't, everyone could do it.

The things that are most worth it generally *are* hard. Meaningful things don't come easy. You'll fail repeatedly in pursuit of something worthwhile, but those failures get you to a place where you can succeed.

Mike, one of my mentors, would always say to me, "Success is not no problems, it is *new* problems." Every time he said that I wanted to throttle him—honestly. But he was entirely right. Every time you grow from a challenge, you know how to manage that challenge—and therefore it isn't a challenge any longer. But the next problem is a new one of first impressions—it is hard because you haven't faced anything like it before. Your success makes the old problems easy to handle, and the new problems are harder simply because you haven't faced them before. Often, I'll get a call from one of the business owners I mentor with a challenge they're facing, and I can spout off some quick advice that can usually easily fix the issue. It isn't because I'm smarter than them—trust me, I'm not—but because I've seen that issue repeatedly and know how to play it out.

Beyond just rational optimism, this is why grit is so critical. Rational optimism allows you to see a viable path forward. Grit allows you to stick to that path when it gets hard. This is where the other tools we talk about throughout the book—the power of yes, the power of no, imposter syndrome as a superpower, among others—get you through to the breakout success. But, just like in the imposter syndrome, you have to be comfortable in the discomfort. You have to know that "hard" is part of the process. You have to embrace the suck at times.

Let's go back to my colleague who celebrates the failure that his daughters experience. He's teaching them daily that success is hard, and it will come with scrapes and bruises and outright failure, and that's not only okay, but it is *good*.

So, when you're feeling like Chicken Little and you think the sky is falling, you can use all the techniques in this chapter, and throughout the book, to manage reasonable awareness of that possibility of failure, or you can embrace the upsides of failure. Or both.

After all, the first year I started the firm, I was sitting with our tax preparer and bemoaning that I had *lost* money with no income whatsoever to show for my hard work. He told me that the statistics showed that most companies lost money before they made money, and that he was convinced that we'd end up as a million-dollar business "someday." I laughed and said I doubted it. Within two years, we were over a million dollars . . . and eventually we were one hundred times bigger than even his big dream for us. Failure begets success. So, it really is okay to fail, Chicken Little. A little bit of rain on your head will make the grass grow.

Part 3

CHANGE THE RULES

The people who are crazy enough to think they can change the world are the ones who do.

—Steve Jobs

7

WORK/LIFE CHAOS

Have you ever noticed that every panel with a woman on it includes a question about work/life balance directed to the woman? Men rarely seem to get that question. I have given talks, been on panels, spoken on podcasts and in webinars for all sorts of audiences and on all sorts of subjects. I cannot think of a single one where I was not asked about work/life balance in some way or another. When I am the only woman on the panel—which happens fairly frequently, given that I work within the defense industry—the question inevitably comes only to me. That the question continues to be asked so consistently is evidence that it is not easily answered; most women (and now, many men too) struggle because our lives aren't set up to allow for easy balance.

In fact, I dislike the term "balance" because it is, quite simply, unattainable. Whoever told us that we could create a balanced life where everything worked in perfect harmony sold us a bill of goods. My life, and the life of everyone I know, often feels like controlled chaos and sometimes not-so-controlled chaos. Sometimes, we can do what we've talked about in the previous two parts of the book and challenge the rules to make your own space within the game. But sometimes, challenging the rules isn't enough. Sometimes, you have to opt out and play an entirely different game.

In either case, I now strive for work/life equilibrium instead. Thinking back to my old science days, there's not technically that big of a difference in the definitions of balance and equilibrium, but it has always felt to me that balance is static—equal force on both sides of a teeter-totter, as it were. Once you reach "balance," there is no movement back and forth, or you become unbalanced.

Equilibrium feels more dynamic—like what happens in osmosis, where the cells continue to cross the barrier routinely but maintain their effective concentration throughout. When a change is introduced, it throws off the equilibrium for a bit until a new equilibrium point is reached, but the biological drive is toward equilibrium being restored, unlike a balance that has no driver toward continued balance. In that, equilibrium is a dynamic process that is never still or silent but always cycling to the desired state.

At this point in my life, I wear a whole lot of really heavy hats—mom to teens, business leader, community leader and nonprofit board member, primary caregiver to two elderly and sick parents, and (certainly not least, although it tends to get the short end of the stick with all other roles) wife to an amazing husband who is the critical secret to keeping everything in some semblance of equilibrium. In my conversations with men and women at varying stages of life from early professional to later life, everyone seems to be experiencing a crisis of balance. Certainly, the pandemic shifts haven't helped, but it seems to be more than that. As a society, we seem to be at a critical juncture where things need to change.

There's an entire genre of books, talks, webinars, and the like—not to mention a massive new executive coaching industry—focused almost entirely on work/life balance as a problem that can be fixed with enough pithy sayings or life hacks. But just like we did with imposter syndrome in chapter 3, I'd like to offer a different take on the concept of balance (or equilibrium) from an Unruly perspective. How can we take the formal rules and the informal rules and change them to get what we need to find our own dynamic equilibrium? And if we can't work within the current rules, how do we advocate for changes in the rules, or how do we decide to play an entirely different game that brings with it the equilibrium we want and need?

Just like everything in our Unruly journey, that's not going to look the same for you as for others, and that's okay. We want to use the Unruly tools to find each of our own paths to optimal equilibrium. That equilibrium will also change over time, not just from person to person, but also as your own life and your own priorities change. Not only is that okay, but it is necessary and unavoidable. And it won't be perfect all the time. If you're anything like me, this will be one of the hardest things to get right. This, more than anything else, takes practice, and self-introspection, and constant reevaluation to get and keep it in some semblance of control.

WELCOME TO THE PANINI GENERATION

In 1981, two social workers coined the term "the sandwich generation" to describe caregivers "sandwiched" between generations—raising kids while simultaneously caring for older relatives. The idea that they were layered like sandwich meat between these two slices of bread—their kids and their parents—seems too quaint an analogy now. Having lived in Italy, I feel much more like the panini; pressed and squished with increasing heat and brute force. But even a panini is only squished from above and below—we almost need a 4D analogy because we're smashed from all directions over long periods of time.

And while the sandwich generation refers only to those who have parents and kids vying for their time, the panini generation considerations are agnostic on what is putting pressure on you. You might not have aging parents or kids, or you might have other considerations entirely. That doesn't mean you're not touched by the panini generation challenges. It doesn't even matter which generation you fall into; there are plenty of Gen Zs who have multiple competing pressures on them, just as many Gen Xs or boomers do. No matter your age, you may still be part of "Generation Panini." Your own panini press may look different than mine, but the same Unruly tools—to include asking the two-year-old's questions, embracing rational optimism, and throwing out the standard playbook, among others—can generally help all of us navigate through our own panini pressures.

Just thinking about all the roles we play can be truly exhausting. I don't know anyone who isn't feeling drained by their multiple hats and high expectations of doing everything "perfectly." And there are no perfect answers, because if there were, we'd have all found them by now. But there are ways of engaging in these panini pressures more or less effectively to find your own right equilibrium.

THREE CRITICAL QUESTIONS ABOUT EQUILIBRIUM

Every time I used to get the work/life balance question, I would answer with some flippant version of the "work/life balance is a myth" response. And while that might be true, especially as it has been discussed ad nauseam since the 1980s, it is a horribly unsatisfying and useless answer, beyond making all of us feel better that we're in good company for failing.

I think we've all read or heard the different takes on work/life balance. You CAN'T have it all. You CAN have it all, but not all at the same time. Lean in. Lean out. Lean to the left, lean to the right, stand up, sit down, fight, fight, fight! Oh, wait, that might be a cheer from my high school days, but you get the point.

Yes, you will never achieve perfect work/life balance, where everything is in optimal flow, and you are a wonderful parent, spouse, worker, friend, and whatever other role you step into at any and all times. That's an impossible standard, and by attempting to achieve it, you set yourself up for failure across all aspects of your life. The panini press will just get hotter and more pressured.

It is better to look for equilibrium across the aspects that matter to you over a longer period. You will never be in balance across all aspects at all times. You might not even be good at any one of those aspects at any given time. But you *can* find a dynamic equilibrium that works for you, at that moment in time, and then reevaluate regularly. The key is to determine if you are engaging in a viable equilibrium over time that will yield your own version of what you want from your own life. With that, you won't escape the panini press, but possibly your sandwich will taste good and be nutritionally satisfying, at least.

I've started asking myself three questions about equilibrium on a regular basis and forcing myself to give honest answers. If those questions point to the idea that I'm failing—in one or more areas—that's when I need to reassess and make changes.

1. What are the important aspects of my life to me at this point in time?
2. Do I feel like I am failing at one important aspect of my life routinely, across weeks or months?
3. Do I feel like I am failing at every important thing at any given point in time?

These three questions aren't stand-alone; they give us a holistic picture but also may point to exactly where we can make changes when we get a signal that we are out of equilibrium. That picture requires us to identify our own specific priorities and then examines two related questions: Is one thing consistently out of equilibrium that we care about, and/or is everything out of equilibrium? If we can answer in the negative to both of those questions *for those things that are truly our priorities,* then we can call our lives in (relative) dynamic equilibrium. If not, we can determine what is off and try to find some small tweaks or large alterations to get ourselves back in the range where we want to be.

The first question is often the easiest one from which we can find changes that will help keep our equilibrium. If we can honestly look at *what matters most to us,* we can offload the external expectations for anything that doesn't make it onto that ruthlessly curated list. This is where we can get Unruly in our personal lives, because what matters most to us may be very different than the unwritten rules in our communities or extended family. *But you get to set your own priorities,* based on what makes sense to you and the people closest to you.

So many of the expectations from the outside are laid upon us, and we never stop to think about if they really need to be *our* priorities. We compare ourselves and our efforts on everything to others around us, and of course we're going to come up short on the things that aren't high priority to us when they're actively prioritized by others. So even if the parents in your kids' school go all out for Spirit Week, with elaborate costumes for every themed day, you can opt yourself out of the chaos and just find something last minute, or better yet, ask one of the inspired parents to get an extra set of costumes for your kid and call it a day. And while your kids may absolutely be your top priority, *their Spirit Day costumes don't have to be.* You can get very granular with your priorities within the big buckets, and you get to define what matters most to you within those larger groupings. So, your relationship with your spouse might be high on your priority list, but creating a massive Mother's Day or Father's Day extravaganza doesn't have to be.

But then here's the Unruly key. You must get introspective about what really matters to you or matters to someone you care about and want to support (like your kids or your spouse). You might need to do some cognitive behavioral therapy on yourself to de-prioritize some things that you may feel pressure to do. You may have to really examine if something you care about is truly necessary given all your other priorities. And you may need to get ruthless about culling those "nice to do" things to get to your true "must do" things.

Then you have to *own your own priorities* and be comfortable not being perfect, even as you see others around you on Pinterest or Instagram with their kids in head-to-toe adorable cowboy outfits for Cowboy Day or with the ultimate expression of their love for Father's Day. Besides, at this point I've realized that those people professing their perfect love on Instagram are often the ones who end up announcing their less-than-perfect divorce a few years later. So, once you identify the manageable priorities within your critical roles, *and the things that can't be priorities*, you must stop trying to meet those external expectations.

The next set of questions then help you determine how well the equilibrium within your important priorities is working. Again, we know that not every single aspect of your life is going to be working perfectly at every minute of every day, no matter how good you are at planning and managing. Those of us who are type A may have a problem getting our brains around that—we can plan for any contingency and bend things to our will!—but when I start feeling this way, I remind myself of a pithy saying that I've heard repeatedly from my operational military friends:

No plan survives first contact with the enemy.

This doesn't just apply in a military context. And it doesn't mean you shouldn't plan—the plan is what allows you to manage the unexpected, because the rest of it is handled—but we all must be comfortable that things will happen, and we have to adapt to those challenges. Unexpected challenges will be introduced, and the natural push to equilibrium will mean that things shift around to deal with those contingencies. That's equilibrium working as it should!

So, the interrelated questions are simply trying to determine if one critical priority is getting short shrift within the equilibrium you've established—if, for example, you've completely lost any focus on your own health to manage everything else—or if you've totally lost all equilibrium because everything feels out of control at once, even for a fairly short time. Either of those things are red flags that your entire equilibrium needs tweaking.

And how do you go about that? Well, it needs to be an iterative process through those three components of the questions, coupled with the techniques throughout the rest of this chapter. Do you have too many priorities that are just not sustainable? Can you choose to do some of them less well—or not at all? Can you prioritize that thing that is not getting attention by dropping something else down the priority list, even for a short time? Can you delegate, or outsource, or empower someone? Only you can come up with the right answer for yourself at that point in time given your particular current situation, but these questions can help guide some of your own answers.

CONSIDER THIS...

Generally, it is helpful to take the Unruly approach to this panini generation stuff as well—find the rules, written and unwritten, figure out how they really work, and then determine how to make it work for your situation. But in addition to the broad-based Unruly approaches that can help you manage to your own optimal equilibrium, there are some basic practical considerations around the actual rules and the way things are done that may be useful to consider. There is an entire group of books that can be—and have been—written about managing the demands of all the different roles you may play, and I won't attempt to do a deep dive into any of it.

But over the years, I've found a few things that are absolutely critical to account for in your approach. These include some practical written rules-based considerations, finding and using available resources to get you to the way things are really done, and learning how to be an advocate for yourself and your family. It also includes understanding how to balance requirements effectively between everyone in your family and your support network, and how to ask for and receive help most effectively. This is by no means an exhaustive list, but it reflects some of the most common considerations when navigating any of the panini generation challenges.

Let's go back to step one of our Unruly journey. Written rules are the baseline for success in our professional life, and for our other roles, as well. Legal considerations need to be your first step in navigating the panini generation issues. By not having this, you are unintentionally throwing others you love in a state of crisis and chaos that is avoidable. Those legal considerations will differ for each of us and may not need an actual lawyer to draw them up (although some things will), but here are some basic guidelines of what you'll need:

- **Estate planning**: This sounds like a big deal, and it can be when it comes to big estates with lots of tax implications, but at baseline you should have a will that specifies a guardian for your children or other dependents (if you have any), an executor for disposition of your assets and "stuff" that matters to you, and possibly your wishes about funeral preparations, and alternate plans if anyone is unable or unwilling to serve. You may not think you need this when you're young and invincible, but again . . . no plan survives first contact with the enemy. Things happen, and you have to be prepared.

- **Delegation of powers**: There are a number of powers you should ensure have delegation—particularly a medical power of attorney if you become incapacitated. But please note that these powers don't survive death; a power of attorney is helpful to manage end-of-life care but ceases to have any effect upon death.

- **Beneficiaries on accounts**: At minimum, for all accounts (bank, investment, 401(k), etc.) there needs to be a listed "beneficiary upon death" or your estate will go through probate regardless of the existence of estate documentation like wills. These should be reviewed periodically to ensure they're still correct given your current life circumstances.

- **Central repository of everything**: If you die unexpectedly, or your parent passes at some point, you want to be able to find and access everything necessary. Make sure you've provided a list of all your accounts, safe deposit boxes, and critical papers (or an advisor/lawyer/friend who has that) and a way to access them all (passwords, beneficiary-upon-death paperwork, whatever works for your circumstances).

If you find yourself caring for—or looking ahead at potentially caring for—your parents or other older adults, it is critical that you have these uncomfortable conversations early to ensure that they have these things in place *and that they give you access to them* or at least tell you who has them when they're needed. Again, this isn't a place where things have to get very complicated or very expensive, but unless you know the rules yourself, this is a place where I wouldn't try to navigate and learn them on your own. Get the legal paperwork completed by an expert and follow ALL of their instructions to the letter.

RETHINK YOUR RESOURCES

How the game is really played is the next step in the Unruly path, and it matters again in the personal navigation through the panini generation. There are myriad resources out there to help with every type of problem you may be facing, but, like everything else, finding those resources can feel almost impossible, and it is easy to feel avoidant when you most need to take action. Again, Google (and Amazon) can be your friend here—there are generally resources dedicated to anything you may be facing, from issues with child discipline to navigating a new health diagnosis to managing the college application process. If you're not finding the right resources you want, change up your word search. You might have to get really creative and think like a marketer or a researcher or a social worker to get to the right combination of words for your specific circumstance. Some of the best things to come out of our ever-connected social media–driven world are groups dedicated to every possible issue, where you can seek advice from people who have been there and done that. Just like with everything else, you'll need to curate the advice you get from these sources, but they can be an entry point, and they often can be a lifeline as your village or your personal rather than professional kitchen cabinet.

There are a few places that are generally helpful for various issues—although this isn't a comprehensive list, but it can be a good start:

- **Call 211**: This is a phone number set aside by the FTC as a helpline for local resources. It connects you to a specific provider in your community that is set up as the hub for referrals and help. It might be the local United Way or a crisis center, but regardless, it should be a good stop for immediate referrals for almost anything you're facing, including mental health issues, housing support, government and nonprofit resources at the local and national level, or almost anything else you can think of that is social-service based. Additionally, calling 988 gets you to the suicide prevention hotline and also to local resources for mental health services.

- **Administration on Aging**: This is a central hub for any issues you're facing as an elderly individual or as a caregiver for one.

- **Early learning coalitions**: These are usually

county-based resources for childcare and education resources prior to formal elementary school matriculation.

- **Hospital systems**: Many healthcare systems—particularly those that are nonprofit—will have resources for
the community available and may be a good hub for
other community service providers.
- **Local government**: Often your local government—
county, city, town—will have a consolidated list of community resources. Check the websites to start navigating.

Beyond your own searches, the best way to find how to
truly navigate these specific challenges is to leverage experts—
either those who do this for a living or those who are experts
simply because they're currently living it or have managed their
way through it. Just like in your professional kitchen cabinet,
you should include people in your support network for each of
the important areas that you're managing who are currently
going through the same issues and can be your support and
a guide to the current resources. You should include the wise
ones who have navigated through it before and can show you
how they've done it (and that it is possible to survive to the
other side!). You should include the ones who just positively
support you, and the ones who are able to show you the tough
love you need to get things done correctly.

ADVOCATE EFFECTIVELY

As you navigate all these competing priorities, advocacy—just
as we've discussed for professional settings—can be critical.

Particularly in medical situations or in getting services for kids with special needs, family members need an advocate to navigate the system and get the best care. Beyond making sure you're leveraging the appropriate resources, sometimes you just have to get loud and demanding for your loved one (or yourself). Nobody knows or cares about your loved one like you do, and our system is broken enough that nobody has the time or energy to focus the way you will on the minutiae, particularly in the middle of a health or other crisis. This is another place where the Unruly perspective is key—figuring out what the actual rules are and how the game is really played are your first and second steps, and then pushing to find the ways that you can work within those rules to get what you need is the critical next step. And in the case of time-sensitive requirements that can be life and death, you need to act with urgency and sometimes with a loud voice. Certainly, manners and care still matter—you can be an advocate without being a "Karen"—but in the end your loved one's health concerns trump any niceties.

A family that I know well has been one of the best advocates I've ever seen for their child with special needs. My friend Lincoln is now ten years old and was born with a disorder that used to be known simply as "floppy baby syndrome." Most kids with this genetic disorder won't live to see their second birthday. Because of the tireless efforts of Lincoln's amazing parents and his whole care team, he keeps defying the odds, but he needs specialized, round-the-clock care to do so. When Lincoln turned five, he was dropped from his Medicaid plan because it only covered certain disorders after age five, and Lincoln's disorder wasn't listed because almost nobody with his disorder ever lives that long. We all went to work to get his insurance reinstated, and the hospital and care providers continued to provide care during the gap. In the end, it took advocacy all the way up to Tallahassee and DC, with some truly over-and-above work from political staffers on both sides of the aisle who fought to get him what he needed. He got onto a Medicaid waiver program and continued to thrive . . . until his tenth birthday, when a paperwork mix-up at the state Medicaid office caused him to lose insurance again, with no immediate solution in sight. One social worker his parents talked to told them that there was nothing she could do to get him covered on an emergency basis, so either they could pay out of pocket (tens of thousands of dollars, assuming he didn't need to be hospitalized during that time) in the gap between coverage, or "I'm sorry, but I guess he'll die." That clearly wasn't acceptable to his parents or any of the rest of us who loved him, so we again went to work to get visibility at the highest levels, and we got all the care providers to allow for a delay in payment while still providing services, and within a few days we had his emergency authorization through pressure at the highest levels of the organization.

ASK FOR HELP

Most of us are likely very good at giving help to pretty much everyone who asks and often to people who don't even ask but we can see that they are struggling. But when it comes time to ask for help, we hesitate. I know that I've gotten better about asking for help over the years, sometimes out of sheer necessity, but usually we muddle through on our own or find someone we can pay to do what we need. For me, I don't have a problem delegating, but I do hate to be a burden on others.

Here's the thing. Your friends want to help. They don't know how to help. You've got to ask—for specific, actionable things. "Hey, I am stuck in this meeting, is there any way you can get Johnny from school when you pick up Sally?" "I need to get out of the house and see someone in person who doesn't require anything from me. Can you meet me for a coffee for an hour?"

I've always loved the concept of "extra parents." With little kids, it can mean pitching in and helping with the physical requirements of child minding. But as kids get older, the extra parenting turned into another safe adult to talk to when their actual mom or dad wasn't approachable for them for whatever reason. In my family, that has taken the form of one extra mommy who has a months'-long unbroken Snapchat streak with my daughter, but also steps in to manage fraught situations when my daughter and I are butting heads too much. And my adult niece, who steps in to take my daughter shopping for homecoming dresses because she's *so much* cooler than I am with a *much* better fashion sense and dramatically more patience. Or my good friend's oldest son, who takes my younger son to play hockey but also gives him sage advice (which, truth be told, is sometimes planted and curated by me) on how to navigate his teen years.

Beyond outside help, it is critical to find the split of duties in your own family that is fair and takes advantage of each person's strengths to the extent possible. That split will look different in every situation, and no way of doing things is necessarily right or wrong—as long as it feels generally fair to everyone.

(Or as unfair to everyone, because some of these duties aren't fun and nobody wants to do them!)

I had been hearing the term "mental load of motherhood" repeatedly, and quite honestly, I didn't fully understand it. This is the idea that moms—but not dads—have to direct everything that happens and keep the balls in the air. Even if the dad takes on certain tasks, the idea is that the mom must stay on top of all the tasks and direct everything. I am fortunate in that my husband doesn't do this; he owns whatever task he takes, start to finish. For example, he manages my son's hockey schedule, and he makes sure he's where he needs to be, while I manage my daughter's hockey, which works out well overall.

I truly didn't understand this mental load concept until it came time to help my parents as their health declined. For any number of reasons—legal paperwork, geography, knowledge of the medical system—I became the default child. That made sense, but what happened was that my brothers didn't feel able to jump in and take whole things off my plate because I was the designated point person. When I would ask them to handle something, they wouldn't be able to, which frustrated both me and them. There was always a valid reason that I was better at everything, which meant that I continued to be the default for everything (even the low-stakes things). And certainly, when there was an emergency, I was the natural option, even when it wasn't any more convenient for me than it was for them.

Over years of conversations, we've come to understand the perspectives of the other siblings; I understand their frustration that our roles are unbalanced in terms of decision-making, and how being cut out of the legal paperwork made them feel, and they understand that I feel overburdened, and they truly do want to help share that load with me. Being heard is central to avoiding—to the extent possible, particularly in stressful situations—the knockdown, drag-out fights that result as the pressure builds and eventually needs release. Beyond just feeling heard, though, we talk about specific tasks that they can own from start to finish, so I don't have to be involved at all.

It isn't perfect. They still say I'm bossy and controlling (and I probably am), and I still feel resentful of the fact that I'm the one who handles most things that come up daily and certainly in emergencies, but the conversations help . . . and asking them to take on projects start to finish has been a game changer.

STOP WITH THE GUILT, ALREADY

There is nobody who can do guilt like a Jewish mother. Since I am both a Jewish mother and I have a Jewish mother, I live and breathe guilt. I bathe myself in guilt. I wouldn't know what to do without guilt.

No matter what, I could be doing better. I could do more.

I am, objectively, a very good daughter and caregiver to my parents. By all rights, my dad should have been gone years ago, after his first hip break with ongoing complications; certainly, after his second hip break in as many years, or his broken vertebrae, or repeated pneumonia and collapsed lungs, or any of the other crazy emergencies he's faced, objectively he shouldn't have survived. But through sheer force of will—his and mine—he hasn't only survived but thrived. And, again through sheer force of will, we surrounded my parents with the required help and support to allow them to stay together even in the face of my mom's advanced Alzheimer's disease that includes paranoid delusions and sometimes violent outbursts. I visit them at least once or twice a week, and I drop everything else when necessary.

But.

But every time I go over there, I feel guilt that I haven't been there enough. That I'm not actively engaging with them. That I still haven't gotten through all the videos that I promised to take of my dad telling his stories. That we can't seem to get my dad to gain any weight, and I haven't found him a new physical therapist that he likes after his previous one moved away.

ENOUGH.

I can promise you, there is always something you'll be able to point to that you could have done better. Sure. But only in a world where you have truly unlimited resources of time, money, and most of all energy. Barring your ability to bend the time/space continuum, or some miracle drug you've found that gives you unlimited energy with no side effects and no risk of addiction, you cannot do it all. You simply can't. I don't care what force of will you have. You cannot will away the laws of time and space.

So, just like the equilibrium questions earlier in the chapter, I want you to ask yourself two questions when you find yourself wracked with guilt:

1. In this instance, did I try to act out of love or malice?
2. Given the entirety of the situation, was there something I objectively could have done differently—that I could have known at the time?

I can almost guarantee the answer to the first one—you can pretty easily respond that you were trying to act out of love, even if it didn't always show as love. Unless you are a sociopath, and at that point, you're probably not still reading this book . . . even if you thought that *Unruly* was going to be a guidebook to getting away with breaking the rules with impunity. You might not have always *shown* love perfectly in every interaction—particularly with a surly teenager, trust me—but I can almost certainly say that you aren't acting out of malice in these important relationships.

And as for the second question, you might be able to come up with something that objectively you could have done better or differently even given the pressures you were facing and the knowledge you had at the time, not just in hindsight. Great. That's a learning opportunity for you. But unless you acted out of malice, take the lesson and move on. You did the level best you could have at the time, and that's the best anyone can ask of you. And more importantly, it is the best you can ever ask of yourself.

The same advice about being comfortable with the 80 percent solution rather than the 100 percent solution is just as critical here as in your professional life. Sometimes, perfect matters. Most times, it doesn't. Your kids won't remember if their third birthday party was a blowout success or not, so don't worry about the extravagant theme with the coordinated activities and prizes and gift bags and whatever else is in fashion. And if you're inspired by annual Halloween costumes, by all means go to town . . . but it is perfectly fine if you make a run the day before Halloween and pick the last costume that sort of fits your kid. And it is perfectly fine—trust me—if your hair is a mess most days. Remember the three questions about equilibrium. Pick the things that matter in the moment to get to the A+ and get the passing grade in all else, or completely disengage and don't try to play in the things that you don't have to do at all. Coming from a recovering A+-or-bust student, that's hard, but it is the only way this crazy life will ever work. Choose, and then own the choice and stop with the guilt. You have permission to do this from the ultimate authority in guilt, the Jewish mother.

8

DON'T CLIMB
EVERY MOUNTAIN

Throughout this book, we've been challenging ourselves to grow and expand by pushing hard, but also by being smart and using the Unruly strategies. When you're in growth mode, that focus can take over most other aspects of your life. It is nearly impossible to push to breakout success while keeping everything else in your life in perfect balance. However, accomplishment and success can also become so much of a habit, fed by internal drive, that we don't notice the telltale signs of danger when the equilibrium is swinging wildly.

I really like the concept of "phases" of life, when various things are prioritized differently. In those phases, priorities often shuffle as needs and wants come and go. Making a decision at one point in your life doesn't mean that decision is immutable. With very few exceptions, you can change course. You can change college majors—or even careers in midlife.

You can leave a bad marriage. You can grow out a bad haircut. Life doesn't have to follow one straight path. Sometimes, the most exciting options aren't even a possibility until they present themselves, coalescing out of unrelated circumstances or emerging after hard work. Certainly, the former was true for me when my husband and I relocated to Europe. I never anticipated starting a company before my circumstances made it the most viable option on the table.

I've changed course multiple times in my life. Throughout my young life I was absolutely set on becoming a physician. It was a singular focus, and everything I did was weighed against how that endeavor would help to get me into med school.

When I got to college, my mind was on the track to medical school, except my body wasn't cooperating. I routinely got sick, but not just with regular colds and flu. By the time I was through college, I had been hospitalized at least half a dozen times for pneumonia. Any time I'd get less than a full night's sleep, I was sick for weeks. Decades later, I found out that I had an extremely compromised immune system, which we were then able to treat effectively, but throughout my school years, I had no idea why I was physically so weak. Regardless, it became clear that, while I could handle the academic side of medical school and residency, there was no way I could physically manage the demands, and just before I started studying for my med school entrance exams, I made the decision that I wasn't going to medical school.

So, there I was, with only a few months left of college, and no clear path forward. My biggest driver in making my choice of what I was going to do after college was—no kidding— that I didn't want to wear a suit every day (or ever). Thinking back, that was probably the wrong way to pick a career, but at twenty-one and at the height of the grunge era, it was absolutely what mattered most to me. At one point, a family friend who had run off to join the circus as a trapeze artist almost had me convinced to join the circus for a year. That would have been one heck of a gap year and would have been my first time ever breaking the unwritten rules that I knew I was supposed to follow.

In the end, I looked at my professors at Michigan, not even one of whom wore a suit, and decided that I was going to be a professor. I got into a social psychology PhD program at Dartmouth and headed off to Hanover at twenty-one years old with absolutely no idea of what I was getting myself into. Dartmouth's program was challenging academically, but even more so in many other ways, including the expectations for the type of research you'd do and the type of career you'd have after graduation if you were "successful." I felt I was locked into a career in academia from the outset. I certainly learned lots of lessons at Dartmouth, but one of the most practical ones was I just didn't want to be in academia.

So, near the end of graduate school, I found myself again completely unsure of what I wanted to do next. The expected path in front of me—a postdoctoral researcher and tenure-track professor role—was available and therefore expected of me. But even though all the options were prestigious and should have been exciting, my gut was telling me that this path wasn't for me. At my core, I knew it.

I tried to talk to a few of the professors at Dartmouth, and even the career counselor, who handed me some tiny book about nonacademic careers for PhDs that was entirely unhelpful. I honestly had no idea what someone with a PhD in psychology could do outside of academia. In desperation, I looked up the office phone number of the brother of my on-again, off-again boyfriend. Marc was a brilliant and extremely successful young professor. We had only met once, for maybe five minutes, four years earlier. When he answered the phone, I launched into a breathless introduction.

"Hi this is Andy's friend Lauren and I'm trying to figure out what to do with my life after grad school . . ."

To his credit, he didn't hang up and didn't laugh at me. He let me finish and then take a breath. He listened without judgment and let me talk out my feelings and fears. Then, he did something so simple, yet so meaningful. He gave me permission to walk away from academia without feeling like a failure, when everyone else around me told me that the only reason anyone walked away from a tenure-track position was because they couldn't cut it. In that conversation, one of his insights pierced through my layers of conflict and confusion.

Just because you can do something doesn't mean you have to do it.

Marc gave me permission then, and for two decades before his untimely death, to say no to the path clearly laid in front of me if it wasn't the path I wanted.

He was the first one who quite purposefully set me on the Unruly path.

Later, as the company grew, there were so many times when people would tell us we *had* to climb certain mountains, and that we were *crazy* or *stupid* or *wrong* if we didn't. So many of those assertions were around hypercharged growth strategies and chasing the total revenue number rather than chasing sustainable work with reasonable margins. Or they were about chasing new markets like cyber or space that "everyone" needed to chase to stay relevant.

In one case, another company that we had been working with had grown from a very small business to a large one, doing about $200 million in revenue by 2009 or so. They started a mantra that everyone in the firm was supposed to repeat regularly—1B/13 ("one B, one three"). In other words, from $200 million they were going to grow to a billion dollars in revenue within three to four years. Our mentor in that firm encouraged us to do the same—set clear and compelling stretch revenue targets that became the singular focus of the firm.

We did exactly the opposite. I actively resisted setting any sorts of numerical targets for the firm—revenue, profit, new sales—and instead told our whole team that success was that we continued to grow *sustainably* and that we were able to deliver well over our promises to our clients. The biggest mark of our success would be if we got follow-on or expanded contracts from the same customers, or if our customers reached out to reengage us when they got to a new job. I actively ignored the advice that so many people gave me to try for explosive growth focused on revenue as a primary driver, and instead we focused on a strategic posture of measured, sustainable growth. It was our own Unruly path, and it felt right, and that was all that mattered.

In the end, the 1B/13 firm didn't meet their targets, and frankly they lost their way from what had built them to their initial success in the effort. They eventually sold the company—for a fire-sale price, if the scuttlebutt in the industry is to be believed—and the owner certainly made a ton of money but wasn't nearly as successful (financially or otherwise) as if they hadn't set such an audacious target that drove bad strategy. I was glad that I trusted my gut in blazing our own path, rather than taking the advice of the mentors from that firm.

I learned a lot from watching other firms do well, and many (many) others fail. At a very specific point, we realized that we were finally ready for that hypercharged growth, and it made strategic sense to chase it, but carefully. We set forth a growth strategy—one that still didn't include specific financial targets but a clear and actionable path to significant growth overall—and then consistently blew past those broad-based expectations. We knew that growth out of small business status could be perilous, with most firms that had been successful to that point not being able to make the leap to the next level, but everything we had put in place gave us the confidence that we could do it successfully.

But somewhere in that time, after we had won our really big contract and were on our way to winning another huge set of contracts, I had the same feeling in my gut as I did that day when I called Marc from my apartment in New Hampshire. We had set the strategy for this growth clearly in front of us, and I knew we *could* accomplish it. But I simply didn't want to. As I stood, strategizing at my whiteboard, I found myself writing something in big block letters:

Just because the mountain is in front of you doesn't mean you have to climb it.

I stepped back and took a deep breath. Whoa. I heard Marc's voice in my head, with a new metaphor but the same advice he had given me for years.

I started thinking about the fact that I had climbed every

mountain in front of me since we started the firm. Some objectively weren't mountains, more like rolling hills, barely noticeable; some were huge mountains with shifting rocks that felt darn near impossible to climb, but climb them we had. Some of the mountains seemed massive when we climbed them but were really nothing more than tiny inclines when looking back, because we ended up tackling increasingly bigger and bolder mountains as the challenges and rewards grew. There had been a couple of spots where we took a very small break to catch our breath, but almost inevitably we just kept climbing, because summiting one opened the vision of the next one to climb.

I never stopped to look around at the scenery. I never enjoyed the different flowers, saw the streams or rivers or valleys. A mentor admonished me for years for failing to celebrate our wins, but even with his reminders, I was never good at the celebration. I always just kept focused on the path in front of me, determined to keep going and take one step after the next.

At this turning point in our company history—where we had to climb a much bigger, much more perilous mountain than we had ever attempted before—I took a look around and saw some scenery for the first time. I saw a river I kind of wanted to paddle down and see where it led. I saw some beautiful cliffs heading down to the water, with trees and rocks and waves crashing, and I wanted to sit and listen to them for a while.

This was clearly a metaphor, but it was also very much a physical reality; just days after the time spent in front of my whiteboard, as I was facing this huge turning point for our firm, my family traveled to Northern Michigan where I had spent my childhood summers. During this visit, as the company sat on this precipice of astounding growth, I looked at this scenery that had defined so much of my early childhood, and I realized that there was so much that I was missing in my relentless drive to just keep climbing. I realized I wanted to try to paddle down a river, or hike into a valley, or just (gasp!) sit and read a book in the woods. It was the first time in decades that I took a few days and drew a no-kidding deep breath.

Kari is another great example of finding that new path. She had been a successful working actress from childhood. But, like so many working artists, she found that she needed to branch out from just acting—and later directing—to settle into a life she wanted. So, she looked at what talents she had from acting, and looked to see where else they would be useful. She taught an improv class to MBA students, which became one of the most popular courses in the course catalog, and certainly one of the most useful. What business leader doesn't need to learn how to react on the fly? And she branched out to marketing—because who is better at marketing than an actress? She found herself working in an area of airport marketing that has strict FAA oversight. Without a template or a best practice to document her airport's adherence to the program, she went back to her theater roots. Taking the process used to reconcile marketing expenditures to theatrical productions (a skill she learned promoting live entertainment), she created a system that dozens of airports use today. She leveraged that synthesis of experience and created her own marketing firm where she calls herself the "Chief Flying Squirrel." And she still gets to act and direct occasionally, because it is her passion, but she makes a living by taking the Unruly path to combining her talents into business-focused work.

LINES IN THE WATER

I think of optionality as having multiple fishing lines in the water; they give you a better chance at catching a big fish. Having multiple lines in play at the same time offers multiple options of possibility that can lead to success. What you do and how these lines are engaged can inform the viability of those options. Every day there are decisions, some big and some small.

But I also make a distinction between **decision points** and **choice points** in my mind. Decision points are binary and often time-pressured. You take the job or don't take the job. You say yes or no to the marriage proposal. You choose which college to go to and make a commitment. Even decisions like these aren't immutable, but they'll take time and effort to unwind, and they can feel life-changing, because they often are.

Before you get to the decision points, however, you get to choice points, where there are decisions to make about foreclosing some options and leaving others open. But those choice points are very rarely immediate and binary. With choice points, you can leave multiple options open and choose which ones to foreclose altogether, which ones to keep "warm" in case other options don't work out, and which ones to actively pursue. Using an example of college admissions, a choice point may be that you winnow down dozens of colleges on your preliminary list to the ten applications that you'll submit. You've managed your resources (time, financial costs of application fees), weighed the expectations for success (safety schools and reach schools) and set forth the best options to keep open. You may know your preferred path—your dream school—and you will put more resources against that option to try to make it work, and that will be your absolute choice if you get in. But you need to have other options open until you know that your preferred path is viable—and that, in the end, it is the path you want to take.

When casting out all these lines in the water, brainstorm and sketch out all the paths you could take at that specific point, no matter how crazy they seem. After the initial brainstorming session, pick the top five to eight options that make the most sense. Write those options across the top (I find it helpful to have a massive whiteboard for this exercise) and follow a few steps forward for each option. Mapping it out this way allows you to see the two to three preferred paths that get you to the right outcome, with probably a few hybrid solutions that combine pieces of those separate paths. It also often shows where there will be specific choice points when it will be best to foreclose some specific options while keeping a few others open—even as you decide to pursue the preferred path—and also where there will be actual binary decision points. Redo this exercise frequently as new information—and new options that you hadn't even conceived of—comes up to allow you to more quickly incorporate developing ideas and data.

At this point in our corporate story, I had come to one of the biggest choice points to date and realized that my clear, preferred path was to sell the firm. While my time at the blank whiteboard made me stop and listen to myself, it had been clear for some time that continuing the same path wasn't going to work for much longer. My parents' health had been failing, and I was spending more time managing everything for them. My kids were getting bigger, and I realized that the "bigger kids, bigger problems" truism really did mean that they needed me more as teenagers than they did as toddlers. I had been neglecting my own health—which was less than optimal even when I was completely on top of it—and my poor husband was a total afterthought. And my cousin Jamie's glioblastoma diagnosis really threw me. He and I had been in lockstep for pretty much our entire lives, not only on the standard life markers—born two and a half months apart, weddings three and a half months apart, kids all around the same age—but also the way we viewed life and family and achievement. His epiphanies about life after a cancer diagnosis became my own in many ways, and I wasn't content to just put my head down and make it work when it was no longer working for me.

I knew that the status quo of staying the CEO and continuing to build the firm to the $250 million/$500 million/$1 billion megafirm track wasn't going to work for me. But, when I came back to that blank whiteboard after my trip to Michigan for a lines-in-the-water exercise, I drew out the other options—hiring a new CEO, promoting someone from within, even taking on outside investors who would bring in their own leadership team—that could possibly get us to the outcome we wanted, even though I was pretty sure the "best" path was going to be to sell.

Why would I do that? If I knew I wanted the sale, why wouldn't I pursue that with a singular focus and make it happen?

Back to the "burn your boat" metaphor—that to get to where you want to be, you need to make a decision and "burn the boat" that got you there so you have no choice but to continue on that path. I have always cringed at that advice, because it is the exact opposite of optionality, and it leaves you over-whelmingly vulnerable to failure without clear options back to success. Should you commit actively and enthusiastically to a path and pursue it vigorously? Absolutely. Should you burn every other option as a backup to prove to yourself and others your full commitment? Please don't.

In other words, if you foreclose all other options to pursue your chosen path, if something blocks that path at all, you're pretty well screwed. You can try to zig right, or zag left, but without keeping those left and right options, you can find yourself marooned without a way back. In our case, if a sale was all we pursued, if anything went wrong in the sale process (and it did—again and again), we still would have been forced into the sale, and we would have found ourselves in a fire-sale position.

So, we kept some of the other options open, literally until the wire hit our bank accounts on the day of sale. What that meant, in practice, was that we didn't follow the conventional wisdom on how to maximize our sale price (and may have left some available money on the table in the sale because of it), but in the long run it was the right thing for me, for our employees, and for the trajectory of the firm post-sale. We kept investing in the long-term health of the firm to allow us to continue running it but also to allow the new firm to be able to continue our growth trajectory unimpeded.

When a friend (and fellow hockey parent), Jeremiah, faced a forced decision point in his life, we ran through the lines-in-the-water exercise to help determine his next steps. In fact, we had run through the same exercise a couple of years before as he was looking at military retirement. At the initial choice point, the path he chose was working for a large consulting firm, but critically, he kept some other lines open in case his first path wasn't the right one in the long run. He was already coming to the conclusion that life in the Big Four consulting firms wasn't for him when his firm did a mass layoff. The generous severance package gave him the space and time he needed to figure out his next option.

Jeremiah had already done some work before he sat down with me for a morning focused on the lines-in-the-water exercise, and he had narrowed his options to his top three, all of which were related—really just different hybrid solutions from the same basic option. Because all the options grew out of a central idea, I asked him to walk me through some other options he had discarded that were unrelated. At least a couple of them were good backup plans, and we decided that he would make sure that he didn't do anything to fully foreclose those options while he pursued his chosen option.

He did everything he needed to activate each of the viable options—taking the initial steps not only for his chosen option but for the low-investment steps to support the backup options as well. As he progressed on the chosen path to a point where he was comfortable that it would work out, he dropped some of the backup options that would have required significant investment of time and resources, but he left open as contingency plans those with low resource requirements. And even better, in pursuing some of those backup options, he made relationships that carried over to his chosen path, which made that path even more viable.

WHEN IS ENOUGH ACTUALLY ENOUGH?

When you put your head down and are climbing every mountain in front of you, the mindset becomes "go, go, go," and taking the path to more and more can become a singular focus. There's always *more* to do. *More* to achieve. *More* to get. And you can keep going and going and *going*, but often something happens to make you stop and ask the question: "When is enough actually enough?"

I've talked throughout the book about finding your breakout success. That takes a drive that looks at every mountain in front of you as the next challenge to conquer. And now I'm telling you that, at some point, you'll get to a time when enough might just be enough. Contradictory, I know. But again, let's look at things as seasons in life. There is absolutely a season where you can and should be pushing boundaries, testing rules, changing the way that success is even defined. Throughout this time, though, you may already be feeling the pull that tells you that you can and maybe should stop taking on the next mountain to climb.

If you're always following the same rules as everyone else, there's no way to distinguish yourself. If you are always looking at the standard path, the same mountain will be in front of you that is in front of everyone else. To get to the breakout success, you need to find a different mountain, or even a river or a stream to paddle down. *Not* climbing the mountain, in the long run, might get you to your desired end result faster or might get you to an entirely different end result that is even better.

And, at some point, particularly after breakout success, you might just come to a point where you want to sit in the crook of a tree and read a book rather than pushing onward. You might want to (gasp!) take a nap. Or play with your kids or grandkids in nature (or in your air-conditioned house). Whether this pause is temporary, or you decide that this is the spot you rest for good, the concept of "enough" becomes a part of that calculation. This is the ultimate Unruly decision, because it throws out all the expectations and rules and gets to the heart of what you really want in your own life.

Obviously, a concept of "enough" comes from a place of at least some privilege. You don't get to step off and relax when you haven't found success in life. But the concept of "enough" can inform almost everyone at most socioeconomic levels beyond basic sustenance. Certainly, money must be a driver of decisions, from a practical perspective if nothing else, but it doesn't have to be the only, or even the most important, driver.

There's nothing wrong with enjoying the fruits of your labor. And while money doesn't buy happiness, it does often buy ease. Outsourcing as much as possible can absolutely help you focus on what really matters, which is key to that work/life chaos management we talked about in the previous chapter.

But as you find success and surround yourself with others finding similar success, at some point striving for more and more turns you into a hamster on a wheel. Excess spending can become the norm. If you're smart from the outset, you will always structure your life to a much lower level of spending than what you're taking in (and what others around you are spending). Even better, if you surround yourself with a mix of people who have found success outside of straight financial success, you'll see a wide range of spending as normal. "Keeping up with the Joneses" becomes less critical when you surround yourself with people who aren't always ahead of you in the socioeconomic realm.

The psychology of "enough" is fascinating. Think about our Neanderthal ancestors. They were programmed for a scarcity mentality—they never knew when their next meal was coming, so they feasted when they had food available—and that's translated to a drive for more than enough all the time in the modern world. It drives our sweet tooth and our obesity epidemic, but it also drives our need for "more" in other arenas too. These drives are inherent in our brains, particularly in the neurotransmitter system for dopamine.

Our Neanderthal ancestors also gave us our need for social support. Our ancestors couldn't survive alone; the worst fate for those ancestors was being ostracized. It was literally a death sentence. This drive for social interaction and social support continues to this day. But that social need also drives comparisons. Some seminal research in psychology in the last century centered around social comparison theory and our drive to compare ourselves to others to determine how we measure up.

Like many of our biological adaptations, our current circumstances changed faster than our genetic code, and some of these adaptations are not well aligned with our current circumstances. Feasting on the easily accessible, calorie-laden food won't help us survive the famine that we likely won't ever face; constantly striving for more success, more recognition, more stuff is a sure recipe for burnout and other mental health challenges like anxiety and depression.

So how do you combat the biological and social drive for *more, more, more* and determine when enough is, well, *enough*?

I have been privy to a number of discussions around the concept of enough versus more when I've talked to business owners thinking about selling their company. Almost inevitably, one of the partners is much more ready for a sale than another one is. Consistently, what I've seen is that the partner who isn't quite ready for the sale will say that they'll be ready once they can reasonably get a specific dollar amount for the sale, and the partner who is ready will then push hard to get to that point. And then the target will move, and move again, and move again. They say they'll stop climbing the mountain once they get to a certain point, but they'll never get there, because they just aren't ready to stop climbing.

There can be any number of viable and valid reasons why you want to keep climbing mountains. There are any number of viable and valid reasons why you want to stop climbing. There is nothing wrong with one person's lack of readiness to step off a mountain-climbing adventure, *unless* the person who wants to step off isn't able to do so. It is only that disconnect that becomes problematic. And it may not just be with business partners and a sale. It can be in any aspect of your life, with those you are close to; it can even be an internal struggle for *yourself* between two competing priorities.

I've found that the best way around these challenges is to use an outside, objective advisor—either a formal mediator or a trusted part of your kitchen cabinet. They can help you focus on the nonnegotiable requirements beyond just money that drive the decision. As with any compromise, hopefully each party will get some of what was important to them and a keen understanding of what each cannot accept. I've played both the mediator and the participant role for multiple discussions using this exercise, and it has been effective every time, across multiple types of decisions.

You can take the exercise in two parts:

1. From a monetary perspective, what do you actually *need*, as a baseline, to get you to where you want to be? Be reasonable about what you need to be happy and comfortable, not what you desire in a perfect world.

2. From a nonmonetary perspective, what are the other nonnegotiables that you need to make your life work? Do you need to lower your stress levels to take care of your health? Do you need more time with your kids? Do you need the prestige of a big title? Be honest with yourself about these nonnegotiables. There's no shame in any of them, as long as they fit within your own values and needs and are true to yourself.

From there, you can brainstorm, by yourself or preferably with members of your kitchen cabinet, options that could drive you to an ideal situation that meets your basic nonnegotiables and your minimum financial requirements, using the lines-in-the-water exercise. In many cases, you might even be able to meet your "nice to haves" and still exceed your minimum financial requirements; in some cases, you'll have to spend some time getting yourself to a better financial position before you can think about meeting the other needs. Regardless, the exercise is useful in clarifying where you want to be and how you might be able to get yourself there.

The concept of "enough" is just one thing to weigh as you look at maximizing your optionality and choosing which mountains and streams to follow throughout your whole journey. But I found that, often, the expectation to climb each mountain in front of you was wrapped up in this drive to continuously get *more, more, more*. It may not be more money, but still, *more* drives us to keep going. It could be more recognition, more power, more prestige. One of the best ways to decide not to climb that next mountain—that you don't have to if you don't want to, at least—is to get comfortable with the idea of *enough*, and to know what your "enough" really is.

9

STEADY THE LADDER

Many, many years ago, there was a very successful and powerful man in a remote village, who was, to be honest, a huge jerk. He had found his great success by himself, or so he believed, and he had no patience for anyone who hadn't found the same success as he had, which is to say, everyone else in the village. He was fond of saying, to anyone who asked, "I did it myself, and everyone else can do whatever they want. It is none of my concern." He lived up on the hill, far away from everyone else, in a beautiful house overlooking the sea, where he never hosted anyone.

Nobody could do anything in the village without him, because he controlled every bit of commerce—the land, the farms, the animals, the shops, the trading relationships; all were owned and controlled by him. Except the boats used for fishing. The fisherman and his family had been making boats by hand for generations, and nobody else in the village knew how to make the boats that would safely sail in the treacherous waters. The fisherman was old, and wise, and beloved by all in the village. One day, when the rich and powerful man had again made life difficult for everyone in the village, just because he could, the villagers went to the old fisherman to complain.

So, the fisherman took the rich and powerful man out on his boat. The rich and powerful man, thinking that the fisherman was finally ready to sell his fishing business, jumped at the chance. They took the boat far out, into the most treacherous of waters. Suddenly, the fisherman pulled out a drill and started to drill a hole in the bottom of the boat, underneath his own seat. The rich man, apoplectic, yelled, "What are you doing, old man? Are you trying to kill us both? You'll sink the boat!" To which the old man replied, "I'm only drilling under my own seat, on a boat I built myself, and I can do whatever I want. It is none of your concern." To which the successful man replied, "Of course it is my concern! We're in the same boat!" At which point, the old man put down his drill and had a very blunt conversation with the successful jerk, who certainly didn't become the nicest person in the village—real life doesn't work like that—but he did start understanding that he had obligations to the rest of the village beyond himself. And when he let his jerky tendencies get the better of him, the old man would show up, drill in hand, and remind him that they were all in the same boat.

Up until this chapter, we've been focused on using the Unruly ways to find personal success. But once you're on the Unruly path, you will see very clearly how the game is structured to be unfair, particularly for those whose fathers and grandfathers weren't able to play that game. The rules, many of which have been in place for generations, have unintended consequences of discrimination. In many cases, to be sure, those consequences historically were the point, rather than accidental. Some of those discriminatory rules are holdovers, and some are actively still enforced to maintain the discrimination. Beyond the rules, there are also unnecessary structural barriers to entry that fall disproportionately on certain groups. Funding sources are not accessible except through closed networks. Mentorship is similarly inaccessible because of those same closed networks. Opportunities for internships—and the ability to work in low-paying feeder positions—are often only available to those with the networks and financial backing to take advantage of those critical possibilities.

For those of us with an Unruly mindset, the next step after our own breakout success should be to reach back and steady the ladder for those coming up after us. We need to make it just a little easier—and sometimes a whole lot easier—for those others than it was for us when we came up. When I'm contemplating the support for the next generation of leaders, I always think of that old carnival game of Jacob's ladder. I personally have never seen anyone succeed in climbing that ladder and winning that prize, except the worker—who would scamper up the ladder with no issues. They learned the way to steady the ladder, and that's great—they could make it to the top. But even when they showed us how they did it, it was still impossible to do it by ourselves. (Trust me, I tried.) Instead of teaching how to climb the purposefully unsteady ladder, let's try reaching out and steadying the ladder. It takes active effort to hold the ladder to make it less treacherous for everyone. And even better, it doesn't take away from our own success to give others an easier path to that success.

In this chapter, we will look systematically at how we might be able to use Unruly tools to upend the game. We'll use the tools from the first section to really understand the rules—and ask the questions about how those rules might impact the fairness of our industry or our world overall. We'll use the Unruly tools from the second section to find the blue water that those coming up behind us, who don't look like everyone else in our industry, can leverage. And then we'll also go deeper into advocacy tools that we mentioned in chapter 1 to change those rules that are hindering progress.

As you navigated your own Unruly path, you may have come across things that seemed to hinder you or others. Or now that you're more successful, you may be mentoring others who run into barriers that you never encountered. Let's catalog those challenges so we can make those meaningful changes for others, not just ourselves. What rules are impacting access? What unintended consequences are there to those rules? Beyond the unintended consequences of existing policies, are there *intended* consequences—in other words, is someone actively trying to create barriers to entry and why? Where do the rules come from and why are they there? And then ask the two-year-old's questions of why those rules are there, and if they really have to be. This is the first task for finding fairness for those coming up after you—look systemically at the way the game is currently being played, and at the rules of that game, and figure out where the problems lie.

Then there are two equally important Unruly paths to upend the game entirely by bringing up the people coming up after you. One of them is relationship based—guiding them in navigating to their own blue ocean through their own Unruly path. The other is changing the system itself. This is the systematic advocacy path that upends the rules—both written and unwritten—to make the entire system more fair for everyone.

Let's look first at our relationship-based ways of steadying the ladder for those behind us.

IT'S NOT EASY BEING GREEN

After a significant drive toward formal DEI (diversity, equity, and inclusion) initiatives over the last decade, there has been a clear backlash in some circles. I have seen a lot of pushback, particularly within the military space. I've heard repeatedly that the military doesn't see color beyond green (the color of the Army uniforms). These folks genuinely, earnestly believe they don't have any bias whatsoever; that they are post-racial, post-gender, post-ethnic beings who treat everyone based solely on valid, objective criteria of merit, and that there are no systemic barriers either.

There is an entire body of psychological literature around inherent biases that has been well documented elsewhere, as well as additional legal literature around the systemic biases that are inherent in our legal and social structures. I am in no way, shape, or form arguing that this literature is anything but clear and compelling. But for sake of argument, let's concede the point for a moment and stipulate that most people don't discriminate, consciously or unconsciously, against underrepresented groups, and that there is no systemic bias that exists because we are finally living in a true meritocracy.

First, we know that this meritocracy has not yielded parity

in the executive leadership ranks or the boardroom, no matter the cause of this underrepresentation. The Conference Board shows that, in 2023, only 32 percent of S&P 500 company boards included women and 25 percent were non-white, and smaller companies had much lower levels of diversity. A Russell Reynolds study published in 2023 similarly found that men are two and a half times more likely to be in executive leadership in the top one hundred of the S&P 500 companies (the S&P 100); only 9 percent of the CEOs of the S&P 100 are women.

Given my discussions with military friends who say they don't see color beyond green, let's look at the military as an exemplar. The military is overrepresented in diversity at the junior levels (particularly in the enlisted ranks), but it has similar issues around senior leadership diversity. So we know that we have not come close to parity in representation at senior levels—regardless whether that's from active discrimination or other reasons. Why does that matter, beyond a basic fairness argument that may not resonate for some?

In one of the most powerful videos I have seen, the then Commander of the Pacific Air Forces who had been nominated to be the Air Force Chief of Staff, now the current Chairman of the Joint Chiefs of Staff, CQ Brown, released a video talking about his experience as a Black man and senior military officer. He said of his military career:

> I'm thinking about my Air Force career, where I was often the only African American in my squadron, or as a senior officer, the only African American in the room. I'm thinking about wearing the same flight suit, with the same wings on my chest as my peers, and then being questioned

by another military member, "Are you a pilot?" I'm thinking about how my comments were perceived to represent
the African American perspective, when it was just my
perspective, informed by being African American . . . I'm
thinking about my mentors, and how I rarely had a mentor
that looked like me. I'm thinking about the pressure I felt
to perform error free, especially for the supervisors I perceived had expected less from me as an African American.
I'm thinking about having to represent by working twice as
hard to prove their expectations and perceptions of African
Americans were invalid . . . Conversely, I'm thinking about
the airmen who don't have a life similar to mine and don't
have to navigate through two worlds. I'm thinking about
how these airmen view racism, where they don't see it as a
problem since it doesn't happen to them or whether they're
empathetic.*

Beyond fairness driving us to ensure that it isn't harder for
remarkable people like General Brown to rise to the leadership ranks, we can look at it simply from a pure business case
perspective. Diversity in our society and our government, in
our industries, and in our own organizations makes clear business sense. Cloverpop has shown, through data gathered in its
cloud-based enterprise decision-making platform, that decision-
making groups with gender, age, and geographic diversity outperform all-male groups by 87 percent, a highly statistically

---

* "What Am I Thinking | General CQ Brown," June 4, 2020, posted
June 5, 2020, by Russell Lewis, MSW, YouTube, https://youtu.be/pfEnYg
3C2JM?si=IkakjHZ-AhfK_MIN.

significant finding.* And in a 2023 study sponsored by Amazon Web Services, researchers at Enterprise Strategy Group found that organizations with mature diversity programs, as compared to their competitors with lower maturity in their diversity programs, were 2.1 times more likely to report beating their competitors to market, grew market share by 51 percent more, and were 2.6 times more likely to exceed their revenue targets by 10 percent or more.† Teams and boards with diversity don't just meet feel-good goals, they lead companies that objectively perform better. And, overall, racial equity translates to larger economic gains as well; according to data from the W. K. Kellogg Foundation, closing the American racial equity gap would translate to a $8 trillion gain in GDP by 2050.‡ We know all of this not because we want it to be true but because research bears it out.

By upending the rules and helping those behind you succeed, particularly if they're not the ones who typically succeed in your industry, you'll widen perspectives and enhance performance and belonging for all. And that, in an ever-more

* "Hacking Diversity with Inclusive Decision-Making," Cloverpop, online PDF, accessed November 13, 2024, https://www.cloverpop.com/hubfs/Whitepapers/Cloverpop_Hacking_Diversity_Inclusive_Decision_Making_White_Paper.pdf.

† Adam DeMattia, "A Mature Approach to Diversity, Equity, and Inclusion Delivers Real Results," Enterprise Strategy Group, March 2023, online PDF, accessed November 13, 2024, https://d1.awsstatic.com/executive-insights/en_US/esgamatureapproachtoDEI.pdf.

‡ Ani Turner, "The Business Case for Racial Equity," W. K. Kellogg Foundation, 2018, online PDF, accessed November 13, 2024, https://wkkf.issuelab.org/resources/30463/30463.pdf.

competitive world, can be your organization's differentiator. This already may be clear and compelling to some of you reading the book, but it bears repeating because it is not something that others have regularly been exposed to, and it is important to recognize when looking at diversity initiatives. That's not to say all diversity programs have been flawless, but we can use an Unruly approach as a different way to tackle some of the unfairness that is clear in the research and hurts individuals, organizations, and our society as a whole.

Now that we understand *why* diversity matters, let's talk about how to use this Unruly approach to upend the game to allow for an effective path for everyone. First, let's look at the individual relationship-based ways to ensure diversity in our own lives, in our own organizations, and in our own industries.

GATEWAY VERSUS GATEKEEPER

"There is a special place in hell for women who don't help other women."

Madeleine Albright had it entirely correct, but I'd expand that to the idea that there's a special place in hell for *people* who don't help other *people*. Especially those who don't help people who don't look exactly like them.

Once you've "made it" in whatever field you have chosen, you can become one of two things—*the gateway or the gatekeeper*. As the gateway, you can be the one who helps bring more people up, over, and through the door for success, seeing a path of abundance for all. Or, as a gatekeeper, you can be the arbiter of who is deserving and block anyone (often who doesn't look or think like you) from coming up behind you.

So often, groups without seats at the table in prior generations had a scarcity mentality, thinking that if they helped others come to the table, there will be less space for them. But this scarcity mentality maintains the status quo. You play into "their" game when you play into the tokenism concept. Success does not have to be a zero-sum game.

Taking an abundance mentality—*there should be room for more at the table, and I'm going to help make that happen*—is the way to change the playing field for the better. And as an added bonus, it gives us better people at the table, with broader perspectives, and that diversity, as we said before, becomes a superpower. So, we find ways to make room. We pull up extra chairs; we build a bigger table. We get creative and throw out the table altogether so more people can join.

I was lucky enough to have one of the very best examples of this mentality from a woman who came out of a generation where scarcity was systemic, and most women truly were hurt in their own career by helping others. Katherine (Kathy) Wallman didn't ever buy into that. She was, when I met her, the chief statistician of the United States. She was a grande dame, with perfectly coiffed white hair, perfectly done subtle makeup, and well-appointed suits. She commanded respect—so much so that the writers for the *West Wing* wrote a side plot in one episode, using her as a brilliant but no-nonsense statistician—and there was nobody in the government that could or would mess with her or her staff.

I had to interview with Kathy as one of the last steps to getting my job at OMB, and I was absolutely terrified. This seemingly perfect, totally intimidating woman walked me into her office, sat me down on the couch, gave me a warm smile, and had the first of probably hundreds of mentoring conversations with me that day. We didn't speak at all about statistics, or policy, or even work, but she invited me to open up about what I wanted out of life and what was holding me back. That day, and for years thereafter (even well after I left OMB), she poured her wisdom and her unconditional support into me, and into everyone else who crossed her path. She gave us all real, actionable advice, and pushed us forward for opportunities. I can easily point to at least a few dozen influential people—titans of industry, cabinet secretaries, White House chiefs of staff, ambassadors—who benefitted directly from her support and sponsorship. She reached back and steadied the ladder for *all* of us, and our country is infinitely better for it.

EXPAND THE SEATING CHART

I know that there have been plenty of times when I've gotten a seat at the table because I'm female. I know there have been more times when I've been excluded from the table because I'm female. Once I realized there was some fairness in the times I was allowed at the table only because I was female, I committed myself to owning my seat at every table I got to, no matter how or why I got there. Sure, I might have gotten there as a quota or a token. Maybe I got there through the generosity of someone else. But I got there, and I was darn well going to prove to them that I deserved to be there, and then that others like me—or not exactly like me or them—deserved to be there as well.

In this journey through military contracting, I was almost always the only woman at every single table, at least as we were getting started. There was one conference in particular, the Special Operations Command industry conference, that was almost comical in the extreme of stereotypes, especially in those early days. My first year at this conference, rumor had it that one of the big investors in some of the guns-and-ammo-type firms was also the owner of some of the large strip clubs in Tampa, and he was using the dancers to staff the booths. There I was, in conservative suits and sensible shoes, and pretty much the only other women at the conference were in bikinis and nine-inch sparkly platform heels. The silver lining was that, for the first time I could remember, there was no line for the women's restroom, but the men's line was constantly spilling out through the convention center. It certainly got better over the decade-plus that I attended, and while there's still not gender parity now, I don't feel nearly as conspicuous as a professional woman at the conference or in the community as a whole.

I was visible within the Special Operations contracting community, even as I was trying to establish myself with a baseline of success in that space, but even more so when we got our first couple of small contracts, and to the extreme once we got our big contract. I was absolutely conscious—even before a misogynist senior program manager told me explicitly while squeezing my arm so hard that he left a handprint—that everyone was watching and waiting for us to screw up. So . . . we didn't screw up. We performed better than anyone else had, so much so that the misogynist begrudgingly admitted our transition from the prior contract was the best one he'd ever seen. We invested more, and worked harder, than any other firm had to for a similar contract win, but it worked. We were at the table, and we proved that we deserved to be there.

The next step was pulling up others after us. We have helped at least half a dozen firms—all minority, veteran, or women owned, and many all three—succeed in spaces that were effectively closed to them. We put them forward for opportunities, we spoke their names in the rooms where we found ourselves. We showed them the pieces that they were missing so that they could own their own seat at the table and prove that *they* deserved to be there.

It is wonderful if you find your way to the table. It is better if you can prove that you deserve to be there. But the real Unruly coup is to make room at that table and bring others to it, so that it starts looking like the rest of society, and everyone deserving can own their own place at a bigger, more effective, and more successful table.

BE THE SHERPA

I've heard plenty of discussions about the differences between mentorship and sponsorship, and why each type of support is critical, particularly for marginalized groups. But I think there is another level of support beyond mentors and sponsors: Sherpas.

Think about the role of Sherpas in climbing the peaks of the Himalayas. They are the ultimate guides because not only have they walked the paths before, but they have the unique tools and tricks to make the path easier than it otherwise would be. They know where the trip wires are and can steer you around them. They can provide you with ways to get prepared for the journey before you set out, so that you're more likely to succeed. But more than anything else, they can get down in the muck with you when things get hard and walk the path with you to get you to your own breakout success.

There's a great parable that I've heard repeatedly that speaks to this concept:

> This guy falls into a hole that is so deep, and the walls are so smooth, that he can't possibly get out on his own. He cries out for help, and a rich man walks by, throws some money down into the hole, tells him to buy a ladder to get out, and walks away. But that didn't help get him out of the hole. The next person walking by is clergy, and he throws down a prayer book and continues on. But that didn't help him get out of the hole either. Then a friend walks by, sees him in the hole, and jumps in. The guy in the hole is incredulous. "Why would you do that? Now we're both down here in the hole!" And the friend says, "But I've been down here before, and I know how to get out."

I met a great guy, who has now become a friend, as he was helping to broker and fund WWC's sale. Maury came up in investment banking as a young Black man who had grown up in the rural South. He told me that the academic side of investment banking, and even the rigors of college and graduate school, wasn't the hard part for him. It was navigating the undercurrent, the social structures, the expected ways of speaking and acting. One thing that struck me is that he said he was with all these kids who grew up going to Montauk for the summer, and he was hindered by not having that shared experience.

But he had people who took him under their wing, and they helped translate for him until he learned the rules of the new game for himself. Sometimes, these were Black men—some of the most recognizable names in the industry—but also some were others who didn't look just like him, but who recognized his remarkable talents. They knew that he needed help navigating and translating in this new world. They became his Sherpas. They had traveled the road already and knew where the challenges were going to be. They knew the places where he wasn't going to know how to handle something and could lead him through it. Maury was overwhelmingly talented and deserved everything that came to him. Nobody handed him anything. But the people who took an interest in him gave him the opportunities to play the game as effectively as the kids who had started out already ahead in the game. Those kids didn't need an external Sherpa to guide them, because their parents, their grandparents, their teachers, and their broader community had been acting as Sherpas to them since birth.

Recently, I was speaking to a group of female entrepreneurs for an event at the technology incubator, Tampa Bay Wave, where I sit on the board. We were talking about how I handled sexism as I was building the company, and I talked about how I used humor to disarm the bullies (with some pointed examples of when it worked well). One of the women pointed out that she—as a woman of color—wouldn't be able to use those same types of jokes without being labeled an "angry Black woman." We all ended up, together, working through how she might approach similar situations given her own social context. Being a Sherpa doesn't mean you've traveled the same path, but as a Sherpa you can use your own expertise and experience to help navigate the new path. Remember—growth is hard, and messy, and can absolutely trigger feelings of imposter syndrome. The same thing applies when you're serving as a Sherpa, but by that point you should be pretty good at navigating through the discomfort and figuring out the best path.

So, in being a Sherpa, we are guiding people through those unwritten norms and expectations. We need to teach them how to approach situations effectively—specifically understanding their own context, not just ours. We can brainstorm with them about how to manage emerging situations, even those situations we've never faced ourselves. We become a critical part of their kitchen cabinet.

UPENDING THE RULES

Now that we've talked about how to steady that ladder for the individuals we have direct relationships with, let's look at more systemic ways that we can use our Unruly tools to change the game for those coming up behind us. How can we make it easier to win at the game that we played, with all the barriers that we ran into? Not by making it easy, and not by giving handouts to anyone, but how can we find the barriers that make it more difficult for some than for others, and how can we level that playing field so that everyone has an equal shot given the same hard work and talent?

Back in chapter 1, we learned some basic tools for making changes to the rules, and we applied them to our own specific situations when there was a barrier to our own success. Now we're going to use those same tools to make systemic changes to address inequities and injustices.

In some cases, your individual advocacy for your own rule changes helped the greater good—think back to Ashley and her efforts to change the rules around the spouse club on base. Her individual advocacy, and her ability to highlight these challenges and make people understand them on a personal level as well as a policy level, got the attention of military leadership outside of the base she was on, and they made policy-level changes to ensure the military policies followed the legal changes in short order. But that happened, also, because Ashley saw that the policy impacted people beyond her and her wife Heather, and she started speaking more broadly to policymakers to tell her story and relate it to the more systemic problems and gaps.

I grew up in a family that regularly engaged in the political process and went to a very politically active university for undergraduate studies, so I've been to my share of protest rallies. They absolutely have their place in rallying the troops, calling attention to issues, and potentially even in changing hearts and minds, which we talked about in chapter 1 as a useful tool in advocacy. And they can often be the catalyst to eventually leveraging Unruly advocacy to make systemic change, but *only* if we take the next step to get the rules themselves changed through our efforts.

Protests can also make people *feel* like they're taking

action, but too often that impact is significantly attenuated. Those rallies, unless they are followed by action to spur rule changes, don't lead to any specific changes that impact day-to-day life. I've always been much more focused on the actual legal and policy changes that will impact the way that the government implements anything. That's leveraging our Unruly tools.

In one great example of the power of a protest rally that actually led to a rule change, when I was still working at OMB, my boss came into my office to tell me that a large group of people in wheelchairs was protesting right outside of our building, shutting down the main street next to the White House. They had gotten themselves out of their wheelchairs and were sitting on the ground and were refusing to get up unless they could speak to the director of OMB about a regulation that they had concerns about. The police, who would normally quickly clear any protest that close to the White House by physically picking up and arresting protestors, were uncomfortable doing the same for people with disabilities, so the director agreed to meet with their leaders.

It was a huge lesson for me on how to creatively upend the typical rules and get your voice heard. Their protest got visibility, and they got their audience with the director of OMB. In the end, the OMB staff were able to incorporate those concerns into the review of the rule changes. So, the protest led directly to an opportunity to change the specific rule that they had identified as problematic.

We talked a bit about individual advocacy in chapter 1, but since we are looking at systemic advocacy, we need to get a bit more systematic in our approach to changing those rules here. When we want to make systemic change, we need to take it in steps:

1. Identify the rule or set of rules (laws, policies, regulations, etc.) that are hindering fair play.
2. Identify and target the organization in control of those rules.
3. Tell a compelling story.
4. Make the ask.
5. Figure out the path to yes.
6. Follow up to make sure the changes are implemented effectively.

Identify the Rule or Set of Rules

As a first step, we need to identify exactly what is hindering full participation and success. Could it be the written rules, or is it some standard playbook-type unwritten rule? What change, or set of changes, would make the game fairer?

To be sure, much of this is multifaceted, and even a set of rule changes won't completely fix the issue. But I'm reminded of my favorite quote by Rabbi Tarfon from around the first century: "It is not your responsibility to complete the work, but neither are you free to desist from it." Just because you can't fix it all doesn't mean you shouldn't try to make meaningful changes and keep moving the needle.

There may be multiple layers of statute and regulation and implementation that impact the fair play of the game. This can absolutely get complex, and you need to understand both the gestalt of the whole and the individual pieces. This change isn't easy, but nothing that matters ever is, is it?

Approach the Organization in Control of the Rules

Once you've identified the rules or set of rules, the next step is to identify who controls those rules. Is this a statutory law passed by Congress (or a state legislature or a local ordinance)? Is it at the regulatory level, where the permissive statute is fine but the way the statute was interpreted is problematic? Or is it a sub-regulatory policy that is enforced by an executive branch agency? Is it just "the way things have always been done" and therefore part of the standard playbook?

Depending on where the rule or policy or guideline lies, you can figure out the best path forward to make changes. You might need to engage in a formal lobbying process to Congress, the White House, or the executive branch agencies. Or you might have to convince the informal power brokers who act as gatekeepers that the standard way can be improved. Knowing *who* you have to convince is the next critical step after identifying what needs to be changed.

This is also where those nontransactional relationships come in very handy. All these decision-makers are just regular people in your community, even if they don't seem like it. Cultivate those relationships before you need them. Help at community events. Go to the events that your elected officials host. Often it is even better to know the staff of the elected officials, since they're the ones making the magic happen behind the scenes.

Tell a Compelling Story

While an argument needs to be legally sufficient, it also needs to be compelling. I've found that the best way to make changes to any rule is to focus both on the actual structural changes but also to *show* people *why* those changes are necessary. Most of us need a framework to hang our understanding of complex issues upon; the story gives us that framework. A compelling story gives us a protagonist that we can all relate to and root for, as well as a clear and easy-to-understand problem that we are trying to solve with the change we're trying to make.

Remember my friend Lincoln from chapter 7? We can—and have—used his story to talk to Florida legislators about the need for Medicaid expansion and perils of the policy that was recently put in place to purge the Medicaid rolls regularly if paperwork is not perfectly in order. Lincoln could easily have died over the gap in coverage that he faced through a paperwork mistake and an uncaring bureaucracy, and one easy way to fix it for Lincoln and kids with complex care needs like him is to ensure that Florida has expanded criteria for children beyond what is baseline required for Medicaid at the state level. In the hospital system for which I sit on the board, we regularly take kids (and their parents) to Tallahassee and DC to tell their stories while we're pushing specifically for changes to the rules that would benefit them directly.

Make the Ask

Once you've made a connection with your compelling story to the right person, make the ask. Know exactly what you're asking for—that you want to change X law in Y way with Z language—and have your leave-behind paper that lays out the ask, the reasons why, and the impact on the person whose story you told (and the many like them).

And a pro tip—think of all of the questions they may ask, or the objections they may make, and have talking points ready to go to counteract those objections or answer the questions. When I'm actively pursuing something as an advocate, I'll often create a Q&A document (like I talked about in chapter 5) and keep it on my desk in case I get a call from someone when I wasn't expecting it. Another pro tip I learned from some media training I did years ago is that you don't always have to answer the question you've been asked. You can always spin it to the answer you want to give. So, "How much would it cost to implement this policy?" can turn into an answer on how costly it would be if the policy weren't implemented, and what eventual cost savings there would be for the new policy, rather than giving an eye-popping number that may shut down the conversation.

Determine the Path to Yes

As we talked about in chapter 4, we don't have to take the first no as anything more than a roadblock. There are almost always additional avenues once you've heard your first no. Can you go to someone else above that first person? Can you find a different path beyond the one you originally identified to make the change? Can you use public pressure? Can you use a different branch of the government to compel that branch you're focused on to make the change?

We found that a well-timed phone call or letter from our congresswoman was often useful to at least get attention from someone higher in an executive branch organization when we knew that we had a compelling argument, and we weren't getting anywhere at the level we were working with. A letter wouldn't do much beyond getting that attention, but if we could use that attention to our advantage, it might be worth it. Or it might just piss them off, which was a big risk of using the legislative route.

Get $h!t Done

Once you get what you want in the regulations, the fight is over, right? Nope, not hardly. As we know from chapter 1, there are levels and layers of policy implementation, and there are also problems of human-centered resistance to change that we need to contend with. Your job doesn't end just because the rules were changed; you'll have to see it through the whole process and use your Unruly tools to work with the policymakers to ensure that the changes are proceeding appropriately and that there aren't additional changes necessary to get you to where you need to be.

FOLLOW YOUR OWN UNRULY PATH

At any point in my life, if you had asked me where I'd be in five years, I would have gotten it wrong by an order of magnitude. I didn't expect to get a PhD until a few months before I started at Dartmouth. I never would have predicted that I would be working at the White House even as I was defending my dissertation. I can confidently say that I never would have dreamed I'd be working every day with Navy SEALs and Army Green Berets. I certainly never would have predicted, even after WWC had been growing steadily for ten-plus years, that we'd reach an annual revenue of $100 million. I wouldn't have said that I'd be on the board of a large health system or writing a book. None of these things were on my bingo card even a few years before they each became a reality.

But through the years, as I've embarked on this Unruly journey and learned how to use the Unruly tools in this book, each of these opportunities presented themselves, and I was able to say yes to each of them. I've gotten to watch so many others embark on their own Unruly journeys and reach to heights that they never dreamed possible. And we've all gotten to do it while solidly playing within the rules themselves and finding our own authentic path to breakout success.

So, take these rules, apply them in your own authentically *you* way, and get Unruly!

Acknowledgments

This Unruly journey has been the ride of a lifetime, and I am so appreciative that I got to experience it with the most supportive village anyone could ask for.

To my husband, who easily represents the best Unruly decision I've ever made. I would not be where I am without your practical support, but also your constant belief in me and your dry sense of humor that made every ridiculous situation more bearable. I will try to listen to all your wild-hare ideas and say yes as often as I can. And to my kids, who have both taken Unruly to new heights. I love that you push the rules . . . although I'd really love it if you would follow OUR rules a bit more closely. Still and all, you are both going places in this world, and I love watching you follow your own mountains and streams. I am so proud and grateful to be your mom. Now, SKATE, SHOOT, and KEEP YOUR STICK ON THE ICE (which is all I really know how to yell during hockey games, and the advice applies to life overall as well). And please, for the love of all that is holy, take your hockey bag out of my car and air it out.

To my brothers, both of whom have put up with the annoying little sister and guided me to be a better professional and (more importantly) a better person, even if you haven't trained the bossy out of me. To my parents, who gave me love and guidance and always believed I could do anything I put my mind to . . . except singing. Everything I've done is possible first and foremost because I had the good fortune to be born to you.

To my extended family, both the Wittenberg and Cohen side, who have taught me to be both witty and gritty. No matter what, there's no family I'd rather have behind me. To my in-laws, who are very possibly the most perfect in-laws ever; supportive and loving without ever second-guessing or judging, and willing to drop everything to come to Grandparents Day even when I forget to tell you until the day of. To my cousins, who were more like siblings, and to my extra mommies and extra siblings who taught me that family was so much more than blood and set the standard for my own cohort of extra mommies and siblings for my own kids.

To my incredible Michigan village, the OG kitchen cabinet of my friends, and the wonderful teachers (particularly Babs, Marla, and JL) who taught me how to think, how to write, how to speak and how to argue, how to stand up for and believe in myself, and how not to take $h!t from anyone. I am grateful to have so many of you still in my kitchen cabinet over (gulp) five decades at this point. And to my Camp Tanuga family, who taught me physical and mental grit but also unconditional acceptance and love. So glad that my happy place became the happy place for my kids.

To the Dartmouth gang, particularly to George (the Ruler of the Island of Misfit Graduate Students) and all my grad school comrades who kept me somewhat stable in the face of utter absurdity. You all gave me the tools, and particularly the unconditional support, to manage even the most outrageous of situations throughout the rest of my life, because nothing could ever be as hard as those four years in Hanover. We can do hard things, indeed.

To my OMB colleagues, who made the eighty-plus-hour weeks enjoyable and guided me through all of my original Unruly paths in work and in life. It still amazes me that a bunch of twenty-somethings were essentially running the government, but we did some darn meaningful work. Grateful that I still get to call so many of you, now around the government and around the world, a core part of my village.

To my amazing WWC colleagues, there's no possible way to express my gratitude for your steadfast commitment to Putting Good Government into Practice, for humoring my hybrid solutions, for buckling in and getting the impossible done over and over and over again. From that first company dinner at Dream View pizzeria with six of us (including husbands) . . . to my final town hall as CEO with hundreds of employees joining from more than fifteen time zones . . . it was a wild ride, and I have every last one of you to thank. I won't thank every one of you individually, or this acknowledgment section would be the size of the book, but I will call out Donna and Heidi. We were the troika of LDH, and WWC became so much more than the sum of all of our parts. I am grateful for your hard work, your friendship, and your counsel over many long years. And thanks, as well, to the Mashantucket Pequot Tribal Nation and the team at Command Holdings for taking what we built and continuing to build upon it with the same care.

To the long-standing mentors and sponsors and Sherpas— particularly Mike and Jake, who were with me every step of the way and were probably the only two people outside of my family who could give me figurative smacks upside the head when I was being stupid and set me back on the right track, which they both had to do way too often. And to Stan, whose advice, counsel, and encouragement was invaluable as I navigated the rules of this entirely new game of writing and publishing.

To my ride or dies, my emotional support ponies, my get-down-in-the-muck crew, my unequivocal cheer squad. You all know exactly who you are and what you've done both when I've been my hot-mess self and when I've gotten the big wins and everything in between. I wouldn't survive a day without each and every one of you.

To my two Nancys—my editor, Nancy Hancock, who has made this book so much more than I ever conceived of when I started this writing journey. Thank you for making sure I'm no longer insufferable and for taking me on an Unruly writing journey. And Nancy Vaughn, who pushed me way out of my comfort zone to expand my platform and audience without ever taking away my own thoughtful authenticity in the process. To Matt Holt and the entire BenBella team, thanks for taking a chance on a brand-new writer.

And to Thea (and Michelle/Jennifer/Melissa before her),

who has the unenviable, and sometimes truly impossible, job of trying to keep me on track and organized.

And finally, to Jamie and Marc and Bill and Reyna. You may not be here with me, but I am trying every day to live up to the Unruly example you each set. You continue to be my guides and my better angels.

About the Author

Lauren **Wittenberg Weiner** became an accidental entrepreneur when she quit her White House job to follow her husband on military orders to Italy. Once there, she was told that military spouses were prohibited from holding professional-level jobs. She started WWC Global, and she and her team grew it to $100 million in annual revenue before selling it to the Mashantucket Pequot Tribal Nation in 2022. In 2018, WWC Global won the largest-ever contract to a woman-owned business in US Special Operations Command headquarters history—the headquarters for the Navy SEALs and Army Green Berets—making WWC Global one of the most successful women-owned small businesses in government contracting. She has an undergraduate degree from the University of Michigan and a PhD in psychology from Dartmouth College. She lives in Tampa Bay with her family, where she sits on the board of multiple non-profits, acts as primary caregiver for her aging parents, and is a loud and proud hockey mom.

Follow Lauren at www.laurenwittenbergweiner.com.